2 95

JESUS *"What Manner of Man Is This?"*

JESUS WHAT MANNER OF MAN IS THIS?

BY RICHARD HANSER

SIMON AND SCHUSTER NEW YORK

Text copyright © 1972 by Richard Hanser
All rights reserved
including the right of reproduction
in whole or in part in any form
Published by Simon and Schuster, Children's Book Division
Rockefeller Center, 630 Fifth Avenue
New York, New York 10020

First Printing

SBN 671-65200-1
Library of Congress Catalog Card Number: 72-82219
Designed by Jack Jaget
Manufactured in the United States of America

This book is for
GRETCHEN

The italic passages in this book are all quotations from the King James Version of The Bible. Some words have been modernized for clarity.

JESUS *"What Manner of Man Is This?"*

PRELUDE

No one who was there on that long-ago Friday, in the city of Jerusalem, suspected what was happening. No one knew that the world would never be the same again.

Outside the Hall of Judgment a mob was howling, "*Crucify him! Crucify him!*" unaware that the words would echo through all the centuries to come. In the face of the uproar, the Roman governor called for a basin of water and publicly washed his hands to show that he, personally, was through with the whole affair. "*I find no fault in this man,*" said Pontius Pilate, the Roman governor. But he gave in to the mob anyway, unaware that the consequences of his weakness would be felt through history forever.

And, of course, the Roman soldiers had no inkling of what they were about when they took him away and scourged him. They beat him with whips until the flesh broke and the blood came, and then they spat at him and made fun of him. To the soldiers, he was just another of those wandering agitators from Galilee, where so many rebels and rabble-rousers came from.

What had the witnesses said against him the night before, at the trial before Pontius Pilate? *"We found this fellow perverting the nation,"* they said, meaning that he was a troublemaker and a threat to Roman rule. *"He stirreth up the people,"* the witnesses said, and such fellows are always dangerous. And what had he himself said, boldly and openly, to the crowds that gathered around him wherever he went? *"I have come to send fire on the earth,"* he said. He was probably crazy, and certainly subversive....

So now, as it was getting on toward noon, they led him away to the killing ground on the outskirts of the city, just beyond the Temple. Golgotha it was called, the "Place of a Skull." None of his followers walked with him as he went to his death. They had all run away, the men who called themselves his disciples. But not the women who loved him.

The women walked toward Golgotha with him, and they wept and mourned aloud for him as they went.

It was a kind of parade, a disorderly death march, that wound its way through the narrow, crooked streets of the old city. The Romans purposely made a spectacle of it. It was a public show that served as a warning to anyone who might be inclined to break the Roman law. An officer was in charge, a centurion with a crested helmet and a scarlet robe falling from his shoulders. A squad of his men tried to keep some sort of order as the procession shouldered and jostled its way through the noonday crowd. The soldiers had more than the condemned preacher from Galilee to guard. Two other criminals, two bandits, were also being taken to their deaths and would be crucified with him.

Some jeered at the prisoners as they went by, but others cursed under their breath or behind their hands at the soldiers. The Romans were in Jerusalem as conquerors, and the soldiers were the visible symbols of the subjugation of the Jews whose city it was. As an added humiliation, the soldiers were only auxiliary troops, Gauls and Greeks and Syrians. This tiny corner of the Roman empire, this outlying province called Judea, was regarded as too insignificant to be worth the attentions of one of the famous Roman Legions. Rome was confident that nothing of importance could possibly happen in Judea.

But of course on that long-ago Friday something of matchless and overwhelming significance did happen there. For generations tens of thousands of pilgrims from all over the world have reverently followed the Via Dolorosa, the way of sorrow, from the Hall of Judgment to the Place of a Skull, the place of crucifixion. But in truth, the way that the preacher from Galilee walked to his death is not known today and cannot be exactly traced. The location of Golgotha is no longer known for certain either, except that it was close by, *nigh unto the city*. But much is known about the gruesome business of executing a man by nailing him to a cross and letting him hang there until he died.

Besides being a horror of bodily pain, crucifixion was designed to be humiliating and degrading as well. It was a punishment inflicted only on the lowest and most vicious of criminals. No Roman citizen was ever sentenced to the cross. Only slaves, foreigners, outcasts and rebels were condemned to it. Crucifixion combined the utmost in cruelty with the utmost in contempt.

Part of the punishment was that the condemned man was forced to carry his own cross to the place of execution. The man from Galilee collapsed along the way, exhausted by the night-long ordeal of his trial and by the bloody scourging that Pilate's soldiers had given him. When he broke down under the weight of the cross, there were no followers, no disciples at his side to offer to relieve him of his burden.

The Roman captain had to order a random bystander to take up the cross and carry it the rest of the way. The bystander was a husky countryman named Simon, from a place called Cyrene, and his chance encounter with that death march on the street in Jerusalem made his name immortal. As long as men tell the story of the man from Galilee, and they will tell it over and over forever, the name of Simon the Cyrenian will be mentioned in it.

And when they were come to the place [of execution], *there they crucified him, and the malefactors, one on the right hand, and the other on the left* ...

All three were stretched along the crosses on the ground, and the Roman soldiers methodically hammered in the long, sharp nails that pinned the hands and feet to the wood. Then the crosses were raised up, and the men hung there to wait through long hours of agony for the only relief that was possible for them, death itself.

Unlike what the paintings, even the greatest, show us, the men were not high up on the cross so that witnesses had to look up at them. The feet of the victims were close to the ground, almost touching it. The men were stripped completely naked to add to the humiliation and to expose to view every twitch and spasm of every tormented nerve and muscle.

The crosses were customarily set up in a place where as many passersby as possible could see for themselves the terrible fate that befell anyone who dared violate the laws of imperial Rome. The man from Galilee hung from a cross set by the side of a road, and *they that passed by railed on him, wagging their heads, and saying, "Save thyself and come down from the cross." And mocking him among themselves, they said:* "*He saved others; himself he cannot save . . .*"

Not many who passed along the road and saw him hanging there knew who he was, but some did. The Chief Priests and Scribes and the Elders knew. They had caused his arrest, and testified against him before Pontius Pilate, and whipped up the mob to howl for his death. They had done it because they hated and feared him. They hated him for the new doctrine he preached, and they feared him for the wonders he performed. Now, in their triumph, they followed him to the Place of a Skull to mock him as he died. The priests and the elders were not the only ones who spoke against him. Others also had turned away from him, saying: "*He hath a devil and is mad.*"

The women who had followed him from Galilee and come with him to Jerusalem stood apart, weeping. They too knew who he was. They knew him as Jesus of Nazareth, and to them he was a prophet, *a teacher come from God*. He had spoken marvelous words of love and revelation to them, and taught them to think and feel in ways that were new and strange. The women of Galilee, and many others who had heard him, never doubted when he said, "*I am come a light into the world, that whosoever believeth on me should not abide in darkness.*"

But now as they stood apart and watched him die, everything he had promised and prophesied seemed to be wiped out and canceled. The light of the world went out for them as they heard his cry from the cross: "*It is finished.*"

But who could have imagined what was beginning? The light that Golgotha seemed to snuff out forever has, instead, been shining steadily for two thousand years. And now, in our time, it is flaring up again in new and surprising ways.

The fire he first cast on his remote and insignificant corner of the earth has burned continually through seventy generations of the family of man. It has spread to every continent and country of our planet. And our own time has seen it carried to the moon.

No other death has ever had such an enormous effect on the human race—on how people live, and act, and think, and talk, and love, and dream, and die. "The most glorious and most terrible deeds of mankind through the centuries," one historian has written, "have all been inspired by the grand and awful symbol of Jesus nailed to the Cross."

Through his dying on it, the cross ceased forever to be an object of horror and loathing and, miraculously, became the universal sign of everything exalted and sublime. Instead of signifying death and disgrace, it came to stand for love, compassion and forgiveness—for the promise of life eternal itself.

It is recorded that when he died there was *darkness over all the land,* and that the earth shook and the graves opened. Many such signs and wonders are associated with his name, and the skeptical have scoffed and turned away from him in disbelief because of them. But no imagined miracle could be more improbable than the actual story of his life and death, and what resulted from them. No king or conqueror, no statesman or scientist, no prophet or philosopher ever changed the world as did the wandering preacher from far-away Galilee, the man known as Jesus of Nazareth.

The man . . . ?

He was that, of course. He walked the dusty roads of

Palestine with his human companions, ate and drank with them, grew tired and slept just as they did. He would sigh, and spit, and grieve, and rejoice, according to the situation in which he found himself. He scolded his disciples when they annoyed him, and sometimes they in turn spoke sharply to him. He was pleased and flattered when women went out of their way to show him attention, and he could weep at the death of a friend. Sometimes people laughed at him, and many of his home-town neighbors, who had watched him grow up, thought very little of him. "Why," they said, "he's only the carpenter, Mary's son. We know him well. . . ." They sniffed at the idea that he was anything special.

Yet those who were closest to him, his disciples, believed him to be not only a great man but much more than a man. *"Thou art the Christ, the Son of the living God,"* Simon Peter said to him, and it was an astonishing thing to say. To call him *the Christ* meant that this Jesus of Nazareth, this carpenter, Mary's son, was the Messiah whom long generations had waited for—the Anointed One, the Redeemer of the world.

It was a great mystery to the men who knew him, and it remains a great mystery. There is no way to explain how it was possible to be man and God at the same time. To be human and divine in one personality. To belong at once to this world and to the world beyond. But that is what millions have believed of Jesus Christ and still do, and what more millions will continue to believe, probably for all time to come.

To the believer it is not myth or fairy tale, but simply the truth, that the long-ago Friday that saw his death on the cross was followed by the glorious Sunday we call Easter, when he rose up from the grave and then ascended into heaven. To the believer all this is nothing more than the fulfillment of what Jesus himself had announced on earth to his disciples and followers: *"I am the resurrection and the life..."*

The power and mystery of this personality, this man-God, has now lasted for twenty centuries, and has renewed its appeal with every generation. The human response to it has run through the whole range of human nature from the sublime to the ridiculous, with every possible variation in between. But the enduring appeal of Jesus Christ has seldom drawn so odd and unexpected a response as in America in our own time.

A line of long-haired, beared and sandaled young people parade under the marquees of pornographic movie houses in Times Square, in the heart of New York City. As they go they chant: *"Jee-*sus! *Jee*-sus! *Jee*-sus!"

They are on television, and an off-screen voice describes what is going on:

"A generation swept by sex and drugs has somehow rediscovered Christ.... Suddenly, mysteriously, God is alive for millions of young people."

The young people marching and shouting under the garish neon signs are "Jesus freaks." They are part of the "Jesus revolution," a groundswell that is engulfing the young from coast to coast. "Jesus people are everywhere, even on Hollywood's Sunset Strip," says another announcer on another program. The "Jesus movement" is news and all the networks cover it. The young now have their own "underground" Jesus newspapers, fifty of them across the country, and they have organized a Jesus news service. Something called the Campus Crusade for Christ sweeps the colleges, and even athletes join it. Football fame and $20,000 a year turn out to be unsatisfying for the first-string defensive tackle of the New York Jets. "I want the fullness of life that Jesus offers," says Steve Thompson, and turns in his uniform. There is a Jesus cheer ("Give me a J, give me an E . . .") and a Jesus sign: a raised arm with the fist clenched but with the index finger pointed upward toward heaven. This indicates that Jesus is the one way to salvation.

In Rome, at the Vatican, Pope Paul VI is baffled when shown pictures of American boys and girls wearing sweat shirts with lettering that says: I LOVE JESUS. The Pope finds this "curious and bizarre." He says, "How all this happens cannot be explained."

Commentators try to explain it by calling it part of youth's revolt against the spiritual barrenness of a materialistic society. In the emotional emptiness of a dehumanized affluence, the young are "turning on to Jesus." They "groove on Christ," many of them, because they have found drugs and rampant sex unsatisfying and meaningless. With the collapse of parental authority and the spread of permissiveness, the young grope for guidance and direction. The home, the school, the church, are not supplying it. Chairman Mao and Che Guevara are remote and dim and alien. But thousands discover Jesus Christ and they find him magically warm, and close, and inspiring.

So with their guitars and drums they begin to play "Jesus rock," and make million-sale hits out of songs like "My Sweet Lord" and "Amazing Grace." The music, says a trade magazine, reflects a growing urge among the young "to establish a rapport with a man called Jesus." The Jesus songs begin to top the rock music charts, and they are heard not only on radio but in night clubs and on television. On Broadway a raucous rock musical called *Jesus Christ Superstar* becomes a smash hit, with tickets selling at $75 a pair when they are available at all. The folk singer Johnny Cash takes a camera crew to the Holy Land to make a film on the life of Jesus, with a blond actor in the title role. But at St. Pius V Catholic Church in Baltimore, young parishioners make Christ into their own image by staining the white marble statues of him black.

In 1971, Jesus Christ is nominated as "The Man of the Year" in *Time* Magazine. . . .

Everywhere, as the 1960s were ending and the 1970s beginning, the figure of Jesus loomed up in areas of American life where it had never been seen before. He became immediate and contemporary. Even amid the most fantastic advances in science and technology that the world had ever seen, his mysterious presence did not dim. It grew. Apollo 11 carried the worship of him into outer space and to another planet.

Edwin ("Buzz") Aldrin, one of the first two men on the moon, took bread and wine with him in little plastic containers. "In the one-sixth gravity of the moon," he reported afterward, "the wine curled slowly and gracefully up the side of the cup. It is interesting to think that the very first liquid ever poured on the moon and the first food eaten there were elements of Holy Communion." There, in the moon module, the twentieth-century astronaut celebrated the Eucharist—two hundred and fifty thousand miles above the earth in outer space. The elements were the same, the sacrament was the same, as when Jesus himself first instituted the rite two thousand years before.

That was in an upper room in Jerusalem, on the eve of Golgotha.

A Eucharist on the moon . . .

It represents a span in time and space and faith that could be considered as much of a miracle as any of the wonders attributed to the man from Galilee when he walked the earth.

Once, the Book tells us, he and his disciples boarded a ship to cross to the other side of a lake. On the way he fell asleep. A great storm came up and the waves filled the ship with water. It was about to founder.

But he continued to sleep on a pillow in the stern of the ship, until the disciples woke him up in panic. They pleaded with him to do something. "Don't you care if we die?" they asked him.

And he arose, and rebuked the wind, and said unto the sea, Peace, be still. And the wind ceased, and there was a great calm.

The amazement of the disciples almost overcame their relief at being saved. They looked at each other in wonder, and asked themselves:

"What manner of man is this . . . ?"

It is a question that has been asked many and many a time since, and it is being heard over and over again today.

THE LEGEND SAYS that at the moment of his birth all nature was stilled.

The birds of the air stopped in their flight. Lambs cavorting on the meadows stood still. Men and women with their arms uplifted did not bring them down. Fawns with their lips to the water refrained from drinking. . . .

Myths and legends cling to every stage of his life, which was like no other life ever lived on earth. Even when all the legends and myths are stripped away and only the hardest evidence is accepted, a great mystery still surrounds him. It begins with his birth.

Although much of mankind has for centuries made his birthday the occasion for its most joyous festival, nobody knows when he was born. The only thing certain about December twenty-fifth as the date of Christ's birth is that it is not the right one.

What happened at Bethlehem on the night we call Christmas is now known around the world, but the first people on earth to hear about it were shepherds. They were keeping watch over their flocks not far from the stable where the newborn baby was being cradled in the straw of a manger (*because there was no room for them at the inn*). When the moment came for the *good tidings of great joy* to be proclaimed to the world from on high, the simple shepherds drowsing among their sheep were chosen to hear the astonishing announcement first.

And when they had seen the baby for themselves, it was they, again, who first spread word of the most tremendous news that anybody ever heard. *They made known abroad the saying which was told them concerning this child.* In the obscure little town called Bethlehem had been born *a Savior, which is Christ the Lord.*

That was long, long ago, and almost nothing in the world is the same now as it was then. But one thing is the same, and that is the weather in the Holy Land of Palestine. December is cold and rainy in and around Bethlehem today, and so it was two thousand years ago. Among the people of the area it was the custom to send their sheep out into the open spaces to graze in the spring. The flocks were kept there until the first wintry temperatures came, with wind, rain and frost. This occurred, as it still does, at the end of October or early in November.

The fact that there were still sheep and shepherds in the fields around Bethlehem when Christ was born means that summer was not yet over. By November at the latest the sheep would have been brought in from the pastures. When December came, there would have been no livestock left on the open plains of Judea. There would have been no shepherds there to hear and spread the good tidings. Christ was not born in December.

Early Christians sometimes observed his birth in January and sometimes in May, but the true day and month were not known then and are not known now. The twenty-fifth of December was apparently settled on because it marks a turning point in the orbit of the earth around the sun. It is the time of the winter solstice, when the sun is at its farthest point south from the equator. With the solstice comes the first turn toward spring. With the solstice comes the promise of warmth and rebirth after the long, deathlike cold of winter.

Long before the birth of Christ the solstice was celebrated as a joyful holiday by pagan people in different parts of the world. But now the turn of the sun toward the renewal and refreshment of the earth is linked with his name for all time. The winter solstice has become a heavenly signal for much of the world to express joy and thanksgiving for what happened in the stable that night at Bethlehem.

Much of the world also keeps track of its historical events by fixing dates according to the year Christ was born: B.C. for "Before Christ" and A.D., or *Anno Domini* —the year of Our Lord—for after his birth. But the exact year, like the day and month, is also uncertain. The date that we use as the beginning of the Christian era, the point in time chosen as the dividing line between B.C. and A.D., is the wrong one.

This is the result of an error in reckoning made by a Scythian monk whose name was Dionysius Exiguus. He was given the task of establishing the year of Christ's birth, which would then mark the start of the Christian epoch in world history. Using various historical clues in the Bible account of the career of Jesus, the good monk arrived at a certain year (754) of the Roman calendar and named it as the one in which Christ was born. The date was accepted, and all the other dates of our era have been based on it since.

But it was later found that there were basic errors in the calculations of Dionysius Exiguus. He had established the wrong year. The result is that the date of Christ's birth is now usually given as B.C. 5—or five years before Christ! To make the matter more confusing, some authorities say the correct year is B.C. 4, while still others say B.C. 6 or 7.

Uncertainty and confusion of that sort surround the founders of other great religions as well. Personalities of the stature of Christ and Buddha and Mohammed take on a kind of mystical vagueness in almost every phase of their lives and characters. What they are, and what they did, is so far out of the ordinary that a kind of unreality and remoteness surrounds them. Even in the features of their lives that they share with everybody else, like birth and death, the record tends to blur and go out of focus. Fantasy and myth alter and color the facts, or blot them out entirely.

Jesus never wrote anything about himself or about anything else, as far as is known. Nothing was ever written about him that can be relied on for at least a generation after his death. There is much about him as a man who lived a life among other men that we would very much like to know, but never will. As the date of his birth is unsure, so is the date of his death. We know little of his boyhood and nothing of his young manhood. We do not know what he looked like. The god in him we cannot grasp. We can only accept it and adore it, or reject it. But even the little we do know about him makes his story as man upon the earth endlessly fascinating. There is no other story like it.

His mother, we know, was a Jewish girl named Mary who was probably no more than fourteen when he was born. This in itself was not unusual. Girls of that age were often fully developed and ready for marriage in the society and in the place where she grew up. But nothing else about the birth of Mary's son was ordinary.

She was engaged, but not yet married, to an older man from her home town of Nazareth, a carpenter named Joseph. In spite of being an unmarried girl who had never "come together" with a man, as the biblical expression has it, she became pregnant. Joseph knew he was not responsible for Mary's condition, and he was distressed when he learned of it. Normally, the situation would have been extremely serious. According to the moral laws of that time and place, an engaged girl who became pregnant by somebody other than the man she intended to marry could have been punished by being stoned to death.

But both Mary and Joseph were assured by angels sent from God that something miraculous was occurring. The child that was growing in Mary's womb had not been conceived in the usual way. The shy and submissive maiden from the unknown village of Nazareth, in the insignificant province of Galilee, had been chosen from among all the women on earth to bring the Son of God into the world. It was the fulfillment of an old prophecy that said: *Behold, a virgin shall be with child, and shall bring forth a son, and they shall call his name Emmanuel, which being interpreted is, God with us.*

Jesus Christ was not the first of whom it was said that he had a divine father instead of a human one. In ancient times, in the East, such stories of miraculous birth were frequent. The philosopher Plato was said to have been fathered by a god, and Alexander the Great as well. Among the Greeks the myth of the demigod Herakles told how he, too, had a natural mother but a supernatural father. There are many more versions of the same story, but none of them is quite like what we are told of the birth of Jesus. None of them tells of God himself coming to earth through the medium of a human mother, and the story of Christ differs in many other ways from the myths that preceded it. All the others have withered into mere footnotes to the past, when they are not forgotten entirely. Only the story of the virgin birth of Jesus has survived and spread through the world, and continues to live.

In our own days, wise men, whom we call scientists instead of Magi, still concern themselves with the remarkable events which are recorded as taking place when Jesus was born. The Star of Bethlehem remains the subject of inquiry and speculation, even in a time as technical and pragmatic as ours. *Lo,* says the original account of it, *the star, which they saw in the east, went before them, till it came and stood where the young child was.* And at Christmastime one thousand nine hundred and seventy-one years later, the leading newspaper of Washington, D.C., sends a reporter to astronomers and space specialists for an explanation of what that strange, new brightness in the sky might have been.

The column-long article that results only confirms what other astronomers have said about the Star of Bethlehem over the centuries. Astronomical calculations have shown that at the time now accepted for Christ's birth, the planets Saturn and Jupiter were in conjunction in the constellation of Pisces, and when planets are aligned in that way they give the appearance of a single bright star.

Or the sign seen in the heavens over Bethlehem that night may have been a *stella nova,* a "new" star that flares up with great brightness and then either dies away or fades out gradually. Or, say our modern astronomers, it could have been a giant comet so distant that it appeared to hang motionless in the sky. The Wise Men from the East, the Magi, could well have thought it a miraculous new star that was fixed in the sky over the crib of the newborn child.

But the star had more than just astronomical interest for the Magi. Those were times of ferment and expectation in that part of the world. Even writers like Horace, Virgil and Tacitus, who had no knowledge of the Bible story, spoke of the strange tremor of anticipation that ran through the people like a fever. There was a widespread feeling that old, old prophecies were about to come true, and that a great redeemer, a deliverer, would soon arise. The feeling was particularly strong in Judea, where prophecies and promises of the Jewish past were well remembered.

The Magi may have been Jewish astrologers from Babylonia, and to them the star was a sign that the Messiah, the long-awaited deliverer of the people of Israel, had come at last. *Where is he that is born King of the Jews?* they asked. *We have seen his star, and are come to worship him.* And when they found him, they fell down and adored him, giving him presents of gold and rare spices and incense.

St. Matthew, who tells the story, does not say how many Wise Men there were, but tradition has made them three and given them names: Gaspar, Melchior and Balthasar. Tradition also says that they came to worship on behalf of the whole of humanity, one of them being black, the second Semitic, and the third representing all the other white races. They did not come with the shepherds while the Holy Family was still sheltered in the stable, as so many painters have pictured the episode. They came weeks later, after Jesus had been circumcised and after his parents had taken him to nearby Jerusalem to present him at the Temple. These were necessary acts that pious Jewish parents would naturally carry out. When they were accomplished, the infant was brought back to Bethlehem. At the adoration of the Magi the Holy Family was living in a house in the village.

We are not given any details of how Mary, the little country girl from Galilee, felt as she saw the gorgeous strangers from the East fall down and worship her baby and spread before him gifts more costly than anything she had ever dreamed of in Nazareth. We are only told that *Mary kept all these things and pondered them in her heart.*

As the angels had instructed her to do, she had named her baby *Yeshua,* or Jesus. It was an old name among her people, and a quite common one. It had a religious meaning: one who saves, a deliverer. The birth and naming of the child had taken place in Bethlehem, and not in Mary's native Nazareth, because of a political development. The Roman emperor had decreed a general taxation and census in the area, and every male was required to go to the place where his family came from and register. For Joseph this had meant a journey to Bethlehem, the little Judean town known as the "House of Bread." It was nestled among the hills five miles south of Jerusalem, and though it was small it was not entirely obscure. Long ago a prophet named Micah had foretold that out of Bethlehem would one day come the ruler of Israel.

But for Mary Bethlehem was not home. Home was Nazareth, a hard, four-day journey to the north—ninety miles over rugged and often desolate country. Joseph would have to walk all the way, of course, and she would have to jog and bump and rock along on a donkey, the way she had come. The way back, though, would be even more difficult and exhausting, for this time there would be the baby to care for and worry about. She no doubt yearned to be safely home and was eager to put the return journey behind her. But it would be longer than she imagined before she saw Nazareth again. The same Magi who had come so far to worship her newborn son had also, unknowingly, put him in danger of his life.

When the Wise Men were searching for the baby Jesus

they made inquiries in Jerusalem, and news of their quest reached the ears of the man who ruled over Judea. This was Herod the Great, a puppet of the Romans, who was insanely jealous of his power and prestige. He had murdered three of his own sons because he feared they were plotting to unseat him from his throne. He strangled his wife Mariamne with his own hands. In the thirty-six years of his reign, hardly a day passed that he did not sentence somebody to death. There was no atrocity too terrible for him to commit when his anger and suspicion were aroused.

The inquiry of the Magi—*Where is he that is born King of the Jews?*—troubled him greatly. He suspected that a rival might be appearing on the scene. This might be a dangerous newcomer who would one day displace him as tetrarch, or governor, of Judea. His priests confirmed his suspicions by telling him of the prophecy that said a new ruler of Israel would come from Bethlehem. So Herod directed the Wise Men to go there and come back and tell him if they found the child. "I, too, wish to worship him," he said. But he meant to kill him.

The Magi, though, returned to their own country by another route without reporting back to Herod. In his fury at being deceived, and in his mounting fear for his throne, he took a frightful vengeance on the town of Bethlehem. He sent in his soldiers with orders to kill every male child of two years and under, down to the smallest infant in its cradle and suckling at its mother's breast. With this general slaughter of the innocents Herod was confident that his potential rival had been eliminated.

But before the tetrarch's killers began their bloody work in Bethlehem, Mary and Joseph had fled to safety with the infant Jesus.

Warned in a dream by an angel, Joseph took Mary and the child into Egypt. It was a refuge for many who had to flee from Herod's wrath. Well-beaten caravan routes led from Palestine across the border and into Egypt. How far into the strange country Joseph took his little family, or where they settled, or how long they stayed—none of this is known. Perhaps they lived from the gold and other gifts that the Magi had left for the child. There was an established colony of Jews in Egypt, so Joseph, Mary and Jesus were able to find shelter among people who spoke their own language and lived and worshiped as they did.

Meanwhile, the old tyrant, Herod, was rotting away from a foul sickness, and he did not survive the massacre of the babes at Bethlehem for long. Murderous to the end, he had his son Antipater killed only five days before he died. At his death there was an outburst of grief from the people—but not for Herod "the Great." The weeping was for the many victims of his long and terrible rule.

Now, once again, an angel of the Lord came to Joseph and told him what he must do: *Arise, and take the young child and his mother, and go into the land of Israel: for they are dead which sought the young child's life.* At last it was possible for Mary to bring her baby safely home.

And home was Nazareth, in Galilee. . . .

It was not much of a town.

Nobody outside Palestine had ever heard of it, and most of those inside Palestine who knew of it did not rate it highly. It was a small hill village, bypassed by the main trade routes. It had no access to the sea, the Mediterranean, which lay not far to the west but might as well have been a thousand miles away.

For long centuries people had been living and working and dying in Nazareth before Jesus came there; but before his coming nothing had ever happened to distinguish it from any of the other little settlements scattered through the area. They had names like Nain and Magdala and Chorazin, and Nazareth's chances of going down in history seemed no better than theirs.

Galilee itself was green and fertile, in pleasant contrast to the harshness and aridity of Judea to the south. It was a place of olive groves and vineyards, of fields and flowers and gardens. Grapes and figs and walnuts flourished the whole year round. Wool came from Judea, but linen came from Galilee.

The people were not always as gentle and agreeable as their surroundings. In the low, rolling hills around Nazareth there were caves, and in the caves there were nests of partisans—"freedom fighters," as they would be called today. They plotted to break the rule of Rome over Palestine, and Galilee was the center of their underground activity. The people among whom Jesus was to grow up were a rugged breed, with a passion for independence and a scorn of authority.

In the more refined and polished centers of Judea, and especially in Jerusalem, they were looked upon as roughnecks, yokels. They spoke a rather crude dialect of their own which everybody outside Galilee recognized at once —and laughed at. The whole province was regarded as a kind of cultural backwoods.

Nazareth, a minor spot even for Galilee, was apparently a standing joke, like Podunk or Ho-Ho-Kus for us. It was hardly a spot where anyone would look for a great prophet to arise. There was, in fact, a derisive saying about the place: *"Can any good thing come out of Nazareth?"*

No sneer was ever more mistaken.

At Nazareth today there is a place called *Ain Maryam*, or Mary's Well. The women of the village have been going there for their water every day for thousands of years, and they still do. It is the same well that Mary went to when she was a young mother and housewife in Nazareth as Jesus was growing up.

The carpenter's trade still flourishes there, too, and visitors find that fitting. Joseph, after all, was a carpenter and walked along the streets with a wood shaving tucked behind his ear, the symbol of his craft. And the streets of Nazareth are where Jesus walked also.

Mary's Well and the carpentry shops are visible reminders that this was the place *where he had been brought up*, as Luke says, and where he spent the formative years of his life. Throughout his ministry the town was linked to his name, and he was known everywhere as *the prophet of Nazareth*. The place he came from was noted even on the sign set over his head as he was dying on the cross: JESUS OF NAZARETH.

But of his life there as a boy and young man, the record says hardly anything. One of the few references comes, again, from Luke: *And the child grew, and waxed strong in spirit, filled with wisdom: and the grace of God was upon him.*

This does not help us much to picture him in his time and setting, or indicate what kind of life he lived as he was growing up. But with clues supplied to us by history and archeology, and by years of scholarly research, many details of the picture can be sketched in. We are not completely ignorant of what life must have been like for a boy in such a town as Nazareth in the time of Jesus.

Nobody would have been very rich there, and the family of Joseph the carpenter certainly was not. When Jesus was presented to the Lord at the Temple in Jerusalem shortly after his birth, the best that Joseph could manage as a sacrifice was *a pair of turtle doves,* or two pigeons. Rich people were required to offer up a lamb on such occasions, but the Law said that God would be satisfied with two pigeons from the poor.

The house he lived in would have been a boxlike affair of clay that was crowded together in an unlovely cluster with other similar ones. His bed would have been a mat on the floor, with his own cloak or a rug to serve as covering. This in itself was not a sign of poverty. It was customary. In towns like Nazareth beds were unknown. Household furniture consisted of a few clay pots, a cushion or two, and perhaps a wooden chest.

His earliest and most lasting memories would have been connected with religion. Some sort of prescribed ritual or observance attended almost every act in a Jewish household of the time. The psalm told them that the Lord was continuously watching them as they lay down and rose up, and as they came and went. He knew everything they thought, said, and did, the psalm said. They believed it. No people were ever more conscious of their relationship to God. The feeling that they were somehow closer to Him than other people governed the whole of their lives.

The first complete sentence that Jesus learned when he progressed beyond baby talk was almost certainly the *Shema Yisroël*, the prayer that every male Jew was required to recite three times a day all his life:

> *Hear, O Israel: The Lord our God is one Lord. And thou shalt love the Lord thy God with all thine heart, and with all thy soul, and with all thy might...*

It was a continual reminder of the Jews to themselves of the creed that set them apart from the people around them. Others—the Romans and the Greeks, the Syrians and Phoenicians—prayed to many different gods and bowed down before idols of wood and stone. But the children of Israel worshiped an invisible God, and one God only: Yahweh, whom we call Jehovah. He was the God of Abraham, Isaac and Jacob, the patriarchs—founders of the Hebrew people and their ancient traditions. Long ago Yahweh had handed down the Ten Commandments to Moses on Mount Sinai, thereby confirming the Hebrews as His chosen people. Had He not, Himself, delivered them from slavery in the land of Egypt and led them into the Promised Land?

At five or six Jesus would have been sent to the local synagogue to begin his schooling. The synagogue was a combination of church, school and community center. It was usually a solid, impressive building, but a plain one without fancy work or decorations of any kind.

School for the young Jesus consisted entirely of lessons

in the Torah, the holy law of God. Day after day the little boys of the town—girls were not included—learned passage after passage of the Scriptures. They recited them together, in unison and in cadence. Word for word, over and over, until the whole class had learned hundreds of passages by heart.

The Scriptures were written in Hebrew, but few spoke that ancient language any more. So the passages to be learned were first read out in the original tongue and then translated into the regional dialect, which was Aramaic. This was a long and laborious process, but it impressed the wisdom of the Torah on young minds as no other method could.

It was the whole of their education. History, geography, literature and, most of all, religion—everything came from the one source, the Scriptures. There were no other books. Jesus, as his later life would show, read the Scriptures in his own way. He saw in them more than a long chronicle of the past and an endless recital of rules and regulations. He saw in them more than anyone else had ever seen.

School and recitation were not his whole life as a boy. Like children of all times and ages, he and his companions had their share of sports and fun. They wrestled and played catch. In town they had games something like hopscotch, as markings on ancient pavements still reveal. In other games, they moved small counters from square to square, as we do when we play Parcheesi or checkers. They got up little shows in which they mimicked the grown-ups by pretending to have feasts and funerals. Jesus, when he grew up, remembered this kind of childhood make-believe and referred to it in one of his parables.

The streets of the town were hardly more than pathways, sometimes paved with stone and often not. There was not much space between the buildings, such as they were. The houses crowded against the shops, and many of the buildings were both house and shop in one. Jesus' house was most likely one of these, with his father's carpentry shop connected with the living quarters.

For the young boys of Nazareth, the town probably held few attractions. But all around it spread fields, streams and mountains, and the sun was warm and bright through the long summers. There would be yellow crocuses and red anemones in the fragrant meadows. Apples and walnuts were within easy reach, and also the red fruit called pomegranate, juicy and pulpy. From the pistachio bushes came little yellowish-white balls of mastic that could be popped into the mouth and ground between the teeth, like chewing gum.

There were mountains all around—large hills, really. In the free hours after synagogue they could be climbed over, and their caves explored. Jesus, we know, had a deep fondness for the mountains of Galilee, and some of the great moments of his life would take place on them.

Within walking distance were other towns. They were much like Nazareth, but being a little way off and therefore a little strange they were attractive to venturesome boys. There was Sepphoris, for instance. It was only three miles to the north, and a garrison of Roman soldiers was stationed there. You could hear the sharp, clear blasts of their trumpets a long way off, and you could watch them drill with their swords and breastplates glittering in the sun.

The hills around Sepphoris were exciting, too, for another reason. They provided both hiding place and headquarters for the Zealots, the guerrillas of the freedom movement. They disappeared into these mountains after delivering their hit-and-run attacks and ambushes. The resistance movement, like everything else the Jews were involved in, had a religious basis. The slogan of the freedom fighters was: "Why recognize Romans as masters when we already have God?"

There is no reason to doubt that the boy Jesus took part in the games and adventures of his young companions, or that he passed a happy childhood. The sayings and stories and parables with which he would one day enthrall his listeners would be colored by his boyhood memories of "smiling Galilee." But as much as he may have been like the other boys of Nazareth in some respects, he was of course profoundly different from all of them. There was, even then, something mysterious and unfathomable about him. What happened when he was still only a boy foreshadowed a future that would set him apart not only from his childhood companions, but from his family as well.

It was the custom of Joseph and Mary to go to Jerusalem every year at the Feast of the Passover. With other devout Jews they visited the Temple to express thanksgiving for the time when, long ago, the angel of the Lord passed over the homes of the Hebrews but slew all the first-born sons of the Egyptians. It was then that Pharaoh, the ruler of Egypt, ended the bondage of the Jews and let them go their own way.

Joseph and Mary took Jesus along to Jerusalem at Passover for the first time when he was twelve. From Nazareth to Jerusalem it was a journey of two or three days, depending on the pace that was set. On this occasion, Mary and Joseph went with a company of kinfolk and acquaintances, so progress both going and coming must have been fairly slow. It was customary to travel in groups, since the roads were often unsafe. There was danger from bandits and roving bands of highwaymen.

The Temple must have been a thrilling sight and an awesome one for a twelve-year-old boy from Nazareth. It was the holiest place on earth, being symbolic of the presence of the most high God among His own people. In a direct heritage back through the centuries it was linked to the greatest and most glorious of Israel's kings, to David and Solomon. In the innermost heart of the Temple was the small, square, empty space that was called the Holy of Holies. It was the dwelling place of Yahweh himself. No one was ever allowed to enter there except the High Priest, and even he could do so only once a year, on the Day of Atonement.

Outside, the Temple was a glittering mass of white marble and gold, with many pillars and courts and porticos. When Jesus first saw it, the structure was still being expanded and improved. It had been rebuilt on an elaborate scale by Herod, whose only rightful claim to the title of "Great" was that he was, indeed, a mighty builder.

Hard by the Temple was the Tower of Antonia, the headquarters of the Roman occupation troops. It included the Hall of Judgment, where one day Jesus would be condemned to death. He must have seen the foreign soldiers marching through the streets and heard the clatter of their arms and the commands of their officers shouted in harsh, military Latin—a foretaste of the impersonal power that would, not far in the future, send him to Golgotha and the cross.

The Temple was always teeming with pilgrims from all over the Near East. Some came from long distances, since half the Jews then in the world lived outside of Palestine. All of them, no matter where they lived, paid a tax of half a shekel to the Temple at Jerusalem every year. It was their central altar, and their only one.

But the Temple was more than a place of worship. It was a kind of supreme court, a forum, and a gathering place of the Hebrew elite as well. The most brilliant and subtle discussions of religious law and practice took place there. Groups of learned doctors continually analyzed and argued over the Law, a theme for endless comment and dispute. There was much about the Temple to enthrall and excite a boy on his first trip from the country. When Mary and Joseph set out on the return journey with the rest of their company, Jesus was not among them. A whole day passed before he was missed.

We are not told why it took so long for his parents to realize that he had been left behind. Perhaps the company of relatives and friends from Nazareth had split up into smaller parties in order to move more freely along the road. Joseph and Mary may have set off from Jerusalem in separate groups. In the confusion of departure, the father assumed that Jesus was with his mother, while Mary believed that the boy was with Joseph. When a check of the company disclosed that he was missing, they immediately turned around and went back to Jerusalem to look for him.

The city was normally crowded enough, with anywhere from fifty thousand to one hundred thousand people squeezed into its narrow streets and winding alleyways. But at the time of a feast such as Passover, the place would be even more clogged and cluttered with humanity. It is not hard to imagine the anxiety of Jesus' parents as they jostled and groped their way through a city that was strange to them, inquiring for their missing child among indifferent passersby. A twelve-year-old gone astray in a big city can be swallowed up without a trace. It was a long time before their search ended.

And it came to pass, that after three days they found him in the Temple, sitting in the midst of the doctors, both hearing them, and asking them questions.

What he was asking the learned doctors must have been very remarkable, because we are told that everyone who heard him was *astonished at his understanding*. He not only asked questions, he also gave startling answers to the questions that were addressed to him. The boy Jesus had progressed far beyond the learn-by-heart schooling of his synagogue in Nazareth. At twelve, he was already asking questions and achieving insights that amazed grown men who spent their lives pondering the Scriptures.

But his mother was more relieved at finding him safe and sound than impressed by his performance before the learned doctors. Like any mother, she promptly began to scold him for getting lost: *"Son, why hast thou thus dealt with us?* [Why did you behave that way?] *Behold, thy father and I have sought thee sorrowing."*

The boy Jesus responded as any son might. He did not like being scolded in public. In all probability it had not been his fault in the first place that he was left behind. So his reply was a little sharp.

"How is it that ye sought me?" he asked. They had brought him to the Temple in the first place, so where else should they have looked for him? He added:

"Wist ye not [didn't you know] *that I must be about my Father's business?"*

Some translations make this reply mean: "You should have known that I would be in my Father's house." Either way, it was his first announcement of his mission on earth. God was his Father, and in his Father's house his work was beginning: the business of examining man's relationship to God, and the saving of men's souls.

His parents did not understand what he meant. But of Mary it is said, again, that *she kept all these sayings in her heart.*

Obedient to his parents now, Jesus returned with them to Nazareth. And again we are told that he *increased in wisdom and stature, and in favor with God and man.*

On this lovely generality, the story of the childhood of

Jesus ends. After the episode in the Temple, where we hear his first spoken words, the record is silent for the next eighteen years of his life.

From the time he was twelve until he was thirty, the biography of Jesus is a complete blank. We do not know what happened in those years. We can only surmise and speculate.

The reason we have no account of it is that none of the four Gospels—Matthew, Mark, Luke and John—tells anything about it. All we know of Jesus, of what he did and said, comes from the four Gospels only. Where they are silent we know nothing for sure. No outside source supplies any reliable information about him. None.

It may seem strange that so great a personality, and events of such significance, could pass totally unnoticed by the world beyond his immediate circle. After all, what Jesus said and did in his own time changed the world for all time afterward. But while he was alive the important events of history seemed to be occurring somewhere else entirely. The death of Caesar Augustus in Rome and the succession of Tiberius as emperor far overshadowed anything that might be going on in a backwater like Palestine. Even there, the appointment of a high priest to the Temple seemed far more worthy of note than the activities of a wandering preacher and his followers. History simply paid no attention to Jesus at the time. He did not seem important enough.

Even the Gospels were not written until many years after Jesus ended his mission on earth. The mystery that surrounds so much of his personality applies to the Gospels as well. Exactly when and where they were written is not known, and may never be. Who wrote them in their present form is also uncertain.

They are derived from eye and ear witnesses who remembered what they had seen and heard of Jesus and passed it on orally to others. At a time and place where books and writing were rare, much of history and most of tradition were preserved and passed on in this way. Memories were trained to absorb and repeat precisely much of what we today leave to books and records. In this way the acts and sayings of Jesus were preserved by his followers and passed on from person to person and from year to year until they were finally written down.

Though they disagree in some incidents and many details, all four Gospels tell essentially the same story. The same picture of Christ and his ministry is drawn in Matthew, Mark and Luke, which contain most of the biographical material we have about Jesus. There are additional incidents in John, but he puts greater emphasis on Jesus as the Messiah and on his divinity.

The Gospels often overlap, repeating the same events and sayings, but each has its own character and style. Each Gospel is presented as *"According to . . ."* Matthew, Mark, Luke or John. So each is colored by the personality of its teller. Matthew is believed to have been a tax collector before he became a disciple of Jesus. Luke was a highly educated man, a physician. Their Gospels reflect their separate personalities, as do those of Mark and John.

In the end, the surprising thing about the Gospels is not that they sometimes disagree, but that they are basically so consistent and that their combined picture of Jesus is so vivid and convincing. They give us an unforgettable character portrait of him simply by telling his story, with little comment and no description.

The Gospels were written to stimulate faith and preserve the teachings of Jesus. The word comes from the Anglo-

Saxon *godspel,* where *god* meant "good" and *spel* stood for "narrative, doctrine, mystery or secret." They were not intended to be history as we use the term. The Gospel writers were not much concerned about the exact time and place of any particular event. They were not reporters with pads and pencils determined to get down every last fact and statistic. They were more interested in spiritual significance than in journalistic detail.

For devout believers, however, the practical problems of how the Gospels came to be written are not important, or even interesting. Christians believe that they were inspired by God and are literally true, like the rest of the Bible. Even so, it is not clear why the gaps appear in the record where they do.

The so-called "hidden years" of Jesus will most likely remain hidden, but it is possible to illuminate them a little. Passages of the Bible dealing with other periods of his life provide some hints, and so does the general history of his time.

Not long after the episode of the Temple, Jesus would have assumed the stature and responsibility of manhood. Like every other Jewish boy, he became legally of age at thirteen. He was now a "son of the Law," a full member of the nation of Israel.

He was also learning his father's trade. It was customary for Jewish boys to learn to work with their hands. Even those who were going to spend their lives studying the Law had to acquire a manual skill with which they could make a living. There is no evidence to support it, but a legend says that Jesus and his father specialized in making wooden plows and yokes for oxen.

If carpentry was indeed Jesus' trade, he seems to have had no passion for it. It is only passingly mentioned in the Gospels. Jesus himself never refers to it. Though he drew many of his parables and similes from the farms and vineyards of Galilee, and from the routine of daily life there, he never used carpentry as an illustration in his teachings.

The word translated as "carpenter" in the Bible may also mean "builder." This would indicate that Jesus and his father worked not only at hammering and planing but in construction. Perhaps they built houses. When he became a preacher he often used figures of speech involving building—the importance of a firm foundation, the laying of a cornerstone, and the like. Carpentry as such did not figure largely in his life or thoughts.

His main interest as he was growing up was certainly the local synagogue. When the time came, he would proclaim his mission there, in the synagogue at Nazareth, where he spent much of his time studying and discussing the Scriptures.

The synagogue was not a church as we understand it. It had no priest or minister. Any man schooled in the Scriptures was free to stand up and comment on the passages of the Law that the *hazzan*, or local teacher, read out. The audience had the right to question the reader and comment, in turn, on the texts. In view of events afterward, we can be sure that the young Jesus carried such discussions into new areas of insight and originality.

From some of his sayings later, it seems clear that he was influenced by the great Rabbi Hillel, who was teaching in Jesus' time. Jesus may well have heard him speak. Hillel formulated a version of the Golden Rule which Jesus himself later preached. "Do not do unto others," the Rabbi said, "as you would not that they should do unto you. This is the whole Law." The sayings of other wise men of Israel also found their echo in the later teachings of Jesus. But when Jesus put his own stamp on them they took on new power and persuasion, and spread around the world.

It would be a mistake, though, to think of him as a

lonely, isolated figure spending all his time brooding over the Scriptures in the synagogue. He was surrounded by a numerous family—brothers and sisters in his own home, and uncles, aunts and cousins scattered about the area.

The Gospels give the names of his four brothers: James, Joses, Simon and Judas (as in Matthew) or Juda (as in Mark). The names of his sisters are not known.

The idea of Mary, the Virgin, giving birth to other children besides Jesus has disturbed many people through the centuries, and many have rejected it. The Greek word usually translated as "brethren" can also mean stepbrother or even cousin. So, it is argued, the relatives described in the New Testament as brothers and sisters were not blood relations at all. They were the children of Joseph by a previous marriage, or perhaps only cousins of Jesus. This explanation makes Jesus the only child of Mary and so sustains her "perpetual virginity," which has always been a cherished element in the worship of millions of Christians, and still is.

At any rate, Jesus' relationship with his immediate kin was not especially warm. His family seems to have been baffled by him, and sometimes even hostile. He must have been too powerful and overwhelming a personality for anyone to live with easily. Genius of any kind can be acutely uncomfortable for lesser folk at close quarters, and Jesus' superiority was both mental and spiritual. His brothers and sisters did not, apparently, know what to make of him. And he, consumed with his sense of mission and aware of the destiny that awaited him, could not be bound by ordinary family ties.

Once, during his ministry, he was told that his mother and brethren were waiting to speak to him. His response was cool. *"Who is my mother?"* he asked. *"And who are my brethren?"* He swept his arm toward his disciples and followers. "These are my mother and my brothers," he said. Everyone who followed his teaching and obeyed the will of God was part of his family. Blood ties and kinship were irrelevant to him. He could be terribly stern on the subject. His teaching would include the hard saying: *"He that loveth father or mother more than me is not worthy of me: and he that loveth son or daughter more than me is not worthy of me."* For him, the love of God transcended all merely human affections.

His brothers, in turn, did not believe in him and his mission when he was alive, and said so. It was this attitude of doubt and rejection among his family and neighbors that prompted Jesus to utter his famous saying:

"A prophet is not without honor, save in his own country and in his own house."

But with his death and resurrection, his brothers changed. They became believers. His brother James rose high in the Christian faith and became head of the Church in Jerusalem. He wrote the Epistle that bears his name in the New Testament.

If we know something of how his brothers felt about Jesus, we know nothing of the feelings of Joseph toward the baffling personality who lived in his household as his son. Perhaps there has been no stranger father-son relationship than that of Joseph and Jesus.

Twice, we are told, an angel appeared to Joseph to give him guidance about the child that would be called his. First he was informed that the child in the womb of his wife-to-be would not be his son (or any other man's, either). Then, in the warning to flee into Egypt, he was again made to understand that a most special fate was reserved for the child, since God Himself was concerned for the child's safety.

Even in the one episode that tells of Joseph's involvement with the growing up of his son, his role is dim. We catch a glimpse of a worried parent concerned about the whereabouts of his son, but that is all. In the search and at the Temple we hear nothing from Joseph. In the sparse dialogue that is recorded, Mary speaks for both of them. Jesus replies to both of them together. He never speaks directly to Joseph then or later.

But what little there is on record about Joseph goes to his credit. Matthew calls him *"a just man,"* and cites his behavior at the time of Mary's pregnancy. Before he was told how she came to be with child, and when he had every reason to believe she had been unfaithful to him, he behaved admirably.

He could have dealt harshly with Mary. He could have had her put to death, as the law then demanded. But he was *not willing to make her a public example.* Instead, *he was minded to put her away privily*—to hush up the whole affair, in other words. It was the impulse of a generous and understanding man, especially in a society that put such a high premium on female chastity.

Even if the Gospels say nothing directly on the subject, perhaps we can conclude that Joseph's attitude toward Jesus was also generous and affectionate. In his teachings, Jesus used the father-son relationship as one of his most frequent illustrations. He repeatedly pictures God not as the awesome and often terrifying Yahweh of the Old Testament, but as "God the Father," with a father's loving attitude toward his children. Jesus himself spoke of his own relationship to God as that of a son to a father. He saw himself as *"the Son of God,"* and generations have called him that since.

The earthly father who loves and forgives his son is one of Jesus' favorite images in his stories and parables. *"If a son shall ask bread of any of you that is a father, will he give him a stone? Or if he ask a fish, will he for a fish give him a serpent?"* Earthly fathers do not behave that way toward their sons, and neither, said Jesus, does our heavenly

Father toward His children. One of Jesus' most famous parables tells of the "prodigal son" who ran away from home and squandered his money in wild living until he had nothing left. Penniless and starving, he comes home expecting to be turned away by his father. Instead, he is joyously welcomed and his father orders that the fatted calf be killed for a feast in his honor.

Such stories suggest that Jesus' memories of his own earthly father must have been warm. Joseph clearly never rebuffed him with a stone when he asked for bread. In Jesus' experience of family life, fathers did not act that way. The loving father welcomed his son home even when the son had *sinned against heaven* and was *no more worthy to be called a son.* Perhaps Joseph was such a father.

But the picture of Joseph remains hazy and incomplete. After the return from the Temple, where his son amazed the doctors, there is no further mention of Joseph at all. Not even his death is recorded. Some time during the "hidden years" of Jesus, he disappears from the story.

Jesus, we are told, *was subjected to his parents,* and this was the customary attitude of all well-behaved Jewish boys in his community. But of course Jesus was not the typical "boy next door," and his relation to the world around him did not conform to the standards that applied to others. Even in his ties to his mother, there was something strange that the Gospels hint at but do not make entirely clear. After the lovely story of his birth, the mother-son relationship seems cool and distant, with one exception.

"Honor thy father and thy mother as the Lord commanded thee" was written in the Law, and he undoubtedly did. After Joseph's passing he had the example of Mary as the custodian of the faith of Israel. It was the mother who largely maintained the ritual in which a Jewish child

was raised. It was she, the mother, who lighted the lamp at the beginning of the Sabbath, signifying the observance peculiar to Jews alone. The Sabbath began at sundown on Friday and continued through the seventh day of the week (Saturday) in accordance with the Book of Genesis, which said *"And God blessed the seventh day"* on which He rested after the creation of the world. The Jews rested too, and did no work on that day.

But if Mary continued faithfully in the old ways, it was the destiny of her son to break away from them and *make all things new*. There was a gap—wider and deeper than what came to be called, long afterward, the generation gap—between him and his mother.

What happened when he emerged from the "hidden years" was so astonishing that many legends grew up to account for what he might have been doing when the record went blank. It was said that he traveled afar, absorbing the mysteries of Egypt and the philosophies of the East. It was also said he took ship for Britain and learned hidden things from the Druid priests, or that he followed the caravan route to Tibet and was taught the spells of the sorcerers there. It is even speculated that during this veiled period he married and had a son.

There is of course not a shred of evidence for any of this. He needed no Druids, or Egyptian mystics, or Tibetan wonder-workers to feed him either ideas or knowledge. There was no trace of any such influence in his teachings when he was ready to reveal them.

And the time for that was swiftly approaching.

On the banks of the River Jordan, in the land of Judea, a new voice was being heard. It was *the voice of one cry-*

ing in the wilderness, "Prepare ye the way of the Lord, make his paths straight."

After a silence of some four hundred years, a prophet had again appeared in Israel. The voice crying in the wilderness sent waves of excitement and hope among the people, for it renewed the ancient promise that the Messiah, the Savior, was coming at last.

But the new prophet on the Jordan was only the herald, the forerunner, of a greater one.

P‍ROPHET WAS A MAGICAL WORD among the Jews. It meant a spokesman for God who could take his place with such giants of the Hebrew past as Isaiah and Jeremiah and Elijah—the thundering preachers who had taught Israel the will of God. The whole moral heritage of Israel was made up of the two elements: *The Law and the Prophets.*

Centuries before Plato, two hundred years before Buddha, a thousand years before Mohammed, the prophets of Israel were teaching the great moral principles that still guide Western man. *My servants,* the God of the Old Testament called them, and in His name they preached ideals and ideas that have been called "the beginning of the spiritual history of the world."

They demanded not only morality among men but justice in society. They spoke for the poor and weak and raged against the rich and powerful. They were the first great social reformers.

They made of Yahweh more than a tribal god limited to a handful of wandering Semite worshipers. They gave Him significance for all people and all time by proclaiming His truths with a passion and an eloquence that made the world listen. To them God was an immediate, living Presence who was constantly concerned with mankind and its doings. He cared about the human race, and expected His creatures to live by His laws.

Prophets by definition see into the future, and in Israel they often made forecasts of things to come. But crystal-ball predictions were not essential to their mission. Moral pronouncements and the summons to righteousness were. Their theme was man's responsibility toward God, and God's ways toward man. In Israel a prophet was one who could use the phrase *Thus saith the Lord* with authority and conviction.

As God's spokesman on earth, the prophet was closer to divinity than other men. Consequently he was held in awe and high esteem among the people. And now a new one had arisen.

His name was John.

He was related to Jesus, their mothers being cousins. They were about the same age, John having been born some six months earlier. It is likely that they knew each other as boys and young men, though there is no record of this. But when John raised his voice in the wilderness, Jesus heard it.

John was in the tradition of the prophets of old. He was stern and hard, and he scorned the ease and convenience of town and city. He raised his voice first at a place called Bethabara, a ford where the winding Jordan could be crossed. It was a wild wasteland there, not far from where the river flowed into the Dead Sea. With the message he brought, and in such a setting, he recalled the fierce and fiery prophet Elijah, whose *word burned like a torch* in calling the people to righteousness and repentance.

Because of the rite he practiced he became known as John the Baptist. Curiously, the Gospels describe him with touches of detail of a kind never accorded to Jesus: He was *clothed with camel's hair, and a leathern girdle about his loins; and his meat was locusts and wild honey.* Dried locusts, sometimes fried in honey, were a common kind of food in that part of the world. The honey could be found in the hollows of trees and rocks, or it may have been a vegetable substance that oozed from fig trees and palms. It was the fare of hermits and holy men, of a man who cared nothing for physical comfort or personal well-being.

Loud and long John the Baptist denounced the moral laxity of the times, calling out to all who came to hear: *"Repent ye: for the kingdom of heaven is at hand."* They came from all around the region of the Jordan, and even from Jerusalem, to hear and be baptized.

For there was a great restlessness in that part of the world, a spreading feeling that something strange and wonderful was about to happen. The times were hard. There was unemployment and much uncertainty about the future. Taxes were high, especially for Jews, who were taxed twice over—by the Romans and for their own religious establishment, the Temple. People were looking for some sign that God himself was about to take a hand in human affairs and change them.

. . . the people were in expectation, and all men mused in their hearts about John, whether he were the Christ or not . . .

The Christ: He would be the Messiah, the Deliverer.

He would liberate the Land of Israel from her conquerors. He would set all things right, punishing the wicked and rewarding the righteous. He would establish a just rule in the world, according to the Law and the Prophets. Peace and justice would prevail everywhere.

But when the prophet on the Jordan was asked, *"Who art thou?"* he answered, *"I am not the Christ."* He said that he was only preparing the way for another—one whose shoelaces he was not worthy to stoop down and untie.

So he continued his call to repentance and baptized many in the River Jordan to wash away their sins. He baptized with water, but he predicted that one was coming who would baptize *with the Holy Ghost* [the Spirit of God] *and with fire.*

When Jesus heard *the voice crying in the wilderness,* he came the long way from Nazareth to the River Jordan. He presented himself to John to be baptized, but John drew back and refused. "It is not right that I should baptize you," said John. "Rather, you should baptize me."

But Jesus insisted, and when the rite, or sacrament, was over, a sign came from heaven. Jesus saw the heavens open and the *Spirit of God descending like a dove, and lighting on him.* He heard a voice from heaven that said: *"This is my beloved Son, in whom I am well pleased."*

The baptism of Jesus was the true beginning of his mission. The vision he saw there confirmed him in his calling. It was an outpouring of strength for his spirit, and from then on he knew what he must do. For those who came to believe in his divinity, it could be said that "the beginning of the salvation of the world" was at Bethabara, on the River Jordan. But an ordeal awaited him before his ministry could actively begin.

From the river he went into the desert of Judea and

there, *with the wild beasts,* he fasted for forty days and forty nights. There he was tempted by the Devil.

To many moderns the idea of a personal devil—a visible, talking Satan—seems incredible. It has a primitive ring, like something that belongs to times far past or to make-believe on the stage as in Marlowe's play and Gounod's opera about Dr. Faust and Mephisto. But the figure of Satan—the personification of evil, the Prince of Darkness—has never entirely faded from human awareness. In fact, it is now looming larger than before in the contemporary imagination.

In California there are cults that chant "Hail Satan!" and perform rites and rituals in his honor. In the industrial town of Vineland in New Jersey, a "sect of Satan worshipers" is uncovered among high-school students, and the death of a local boy is said to be somehow connected with it. Charles Manson, the leader in the frightful Sharon Tate murders, is described in the newspapers as "a self-styled Satanist." The CBS television network runs a five-part series on witchcraft and Satanism on its evening schedule. "Satanism," says the news announcer, "is growing in popularity, especially among the young." In Bible times the belief in devils, angels and evil spirits was universal, and it has obviously not died out entirely, even in the day of television, atomic energy and moon shots.

The tempting of Jesus in the desert can be taken literally, as believers do, or looked upon as an allegory—a story intended to illustrate the mental and spiritual ordeal he passed through to prepare for his mission. In the lives of the great religious innovators the line between reality and allegory and between biography and myth is not always sharply drawn.

There were three temptations for Jesus.

First, the Devil challenged him to prove that he was the son of God by turning the stones of the desert into bread. Famished after his long fast, Jesus might well have used his supernatural powers to supply himself with food. Instead he quoted Scripture: *"Man shall not live by bread alone . . ."* The words he used were an echo from the Old Testament, from the Book of Deuteronomy. His use of them showed how deeply rooted his ministry would be in the ancient faith of the Hebrews. *Not by bread only . . . but by the word of God.* There was more to life, he was saying, than catering to the needs of the body. The things of the spirit were more important. That would be a cardinal point in his teaching.

Next, the Devil took him up a high mountain and *showed unto him all the kingdoms of the world in a moment of time.* All the glory and all the power of those kingdoms would be his if he would only kneel down before Satan. But Jesus was able to resist again. God alone was worthy of worship, he said, not power and not dominion.

Then Jesus was taken to the topmost tower of the Temple in Jerusalem. Surely, said Satan, if he were the Son of God he could throw himself down from even this dizzy height and no harm would come to him. Satan quoted Scripture to assure him that angels would bear him up and prevent him from suffering any harm. . . .

But again Jesus refused to be baited into demonstrating the power that was in him, or making an empty exhibition of his divinity. The strength of heaven was not to be summoned merely for pride or show. He turned away the third temptation by saying to Satan: *"Thou shalt not tempt the Lord thy God."*

So he passed the test, survived the ordeal, and the Devil *departed from him for a season.* "For a season" meant for a time, not forever. Jesus, in his human role, was not finished with temptation and ordeal.

His forty-day fast in the wilderness set the pattern

for generations of Christians who have observed the forty days between Ash Wednesday and Easter as the time of Lent, a time for fasting and penitence. For Jesus the ordeal in the desert was a milestone along his path to fulfillment.

He was now *about thirty years of age,* which is as close as the Gospels ever come to telling us how old he was at any stage of his adult life. The length of the ministry on which he was beginning is uncertain, too. Did he make his enormous impression on the world in less than two years of public activity, as some scholars think? Or was it a full two years? Or three? Or ten? No one knows for sure, since the Bible narratives allow for differing estimates of the time that his mission lasted.

From the Valley of the Jordan he went north into Galilee, to a little town called Cana. It was not far from Nazareth, and his widowed mother may have been living there at the time. At any rate, a reunion between Jesus and Mary took place at Cana. It occurred at a wedding to which he and his mother were invited.

As was customary among the Jews of Galilee, the formal religious ceremony was followed by a feast—a wedding party. Such celebrations might go on for days, with numerous guests, much eating and drinking, and general merriment. For Jesus the contrast must have been very striking—the joy and joking of the wedding feast so soon after the deep solemnity of his baptism and the harsh ordeal in the wilderness.

It was highly significant that he was at the feast at all. It revealed that he would not, in performing his mission, withdraw from society as John the Baptist had done. He would not assume the role of hermit and recluse as the ancient prophets often did. His presence at so festive a gathering showed that he enjoyed mingling with friends and neighbors and would not hold himself aloof from the homey pleasures of everyday life. Far from condemning the merriment around him, he saved the party from collapse—and in a way in which no one but he could possibly have done it.

A crisis arose when his mother came to tell him that the hosts had run out of wine. In translation, the reply that Jesus gave her has a surly ring: *"Woman, what have I to do with thee? My hour has not yet come."*

For whatever reason, Jesus never addressed Mary as "Mother." He spoke to her as "Woman," which has for us a contemptuous sound. But in Aramaic, the language Jesus used, the word is a title of respect, equal to "Madam." He was politely telling his mother that he would act when he was ready. Evidently his reply was understood better by Mary, who heard it, than by us who read it in translation. She was confident that her son would know what should be done. She turned to the servants and asked them to do whatever Jesus might tell them to.

There were six large stone vats in the house where the party was being held. They were used to hold water for the numerous ritual washings that were required in every Jewish household. They held about twenty-five gallons each. Jesus requested the servants to fill the waterpots. *And they filled them up to the brim.*

When this was done, he told the servants to draw off some of the water and take it to the steward who was in charge of the feast. The steward tasted what was brought to him and was amazed. He called the bridegroom over and said: "You've kept the best wine until last! Usually a host serves the good wine first and then, when the guests have had a lot to drink, the poorer wine is brought out. But you've done just the reverse."

Quietly, making no show of it, Jesus had turned the water into wine.

He would perform many other miracles in the future. He would calm a stormy sea. He would walk upon water. He would cure the sick and lame. According to the Gospel, he would even bring the dead back to life. But there was something special and endearing about this first miracle at the wedding in Cana. It was so warm and neighborly. Jesus had kept a party going because his mother asked him to.

What he had done did not go entirely unnoticed among the guests, although he had made no display of it. *This beginning of miracles* caused some who were present to believe in him. They were his first disciples.

Not long after the wedding feast, he showed an entirely different side of himself. It was Passover time again, and he journeyed to Jerusalem.

As usual, the Temple was swarming with pious Jews who pressed and jostled through the open-air courts in a many-colored mob intent on the business of worship. Costumed in every hue and style of the Near East, they came to offer their sacrifices to the One True God. The outer area of the Temple was called the Court of the Gentiles, and this was the busiest spot in Jerusalem at the time of the Passover.

It was more like a bazaar, an open-air market, than a religious quarter. The place was dotted with stalls and booths where noisy disputes and shrill haggling went on continually. Venders hawked the oil and incense needed for the various Temple observances. On sale also were the living creatures which the pilgrims would sacrifice to Yahweh according to the depth of their piety and their purses. They could buy doves, or perhaps a sheep or a ram. Now and then a stately worshiper with a full purse ostentatiously bought an ox. Almost every purchase was accompanied by spirited wrangling over the price.

Since the pilgrims came from different countries, money-changing was one of the liveliest activities in the Court of the Gentiles. Foreign money was considered to be "unclean." Only the currency of the Temple itself could be accepted in the purchase of a sacrifice. The Temple tax, of course, could be paid only in Jewish money. Drachmas and denarii and lepta had to be changed for shekels (which, roughly, were worth about $1.14 in our money today). The money-changers were shrewd, if not sharp, at their business, and they charged a fee for it. The pilgrims could not always be sure they were getting their money's worth in the conversion of their foreign coins into Temple currency.

With their sacrifices bought and paid for, the pilgrims then lined up to await their turn in the Court of the Priests. Here the Altar of Sacrifice was located, and here the ritual killing went on all day long until the place took on the look of a slaughterhouse. Beginning with the haggling at the booths and ending with the cries of the butchered animals, the rite of sacrifice could not have been a very edifying spectacle as practiced in the Temple of Jerusalem.

Jesus did not think it was. Changing money and killing animals was not his idea of how God should be worshiped.

There are legends about his boyhood that tell of an explosive element in his character, of something volcanic. Several of these apocryphal stories are both unattractive and puzzling. They do not fit the picture of Jesus as the world now knows him. Still, the fact that such legends were told at all may be of some significance. As he demonstrated during this Passover at the Temple of Jerusalem, he was capable of acting impetuously and vigorously. He could be violent.

Taking in the scene in the Court of the Gentiles, he acted.

He took a number of cords and braided them together into a scourge, a whip. Flailing to the right and left, he went among the stalls and booths and drove out the dealers and sellers. He overturned the tables of the money-changers, and spilled their coins onto the ground. He drove off the oxen and sheep. "*Take these things hence,*" he said to the dealers in doves, and whipped them out of the Temple area.

"*Make not my Father's house a house of merchandise*" was his order and his warning to the sellers and dealers and money-changers. They had, he said, turned *the house of prayer* into *a den of thieves*. His scourge and his fury in the Court of the Gentiles demonstrated to the world a teaching of his that would become famous: "*No man can serve two masters . . . Ye cannot serve God and mammon* [money, property]."

This confrontation, this physical assault on the system of his time, is the only such episode recorded in his career. Coming at the start of his ministry (according to the Gospel of John*) it could be taken as the act of a crusader going all out into his first battle, aflame with the justice of his cause. The fact that he never repeated such an action indicated that he came to rely on the power of his words, his message, his inspiration, rather than on physical force. The way to alter things was to change men's minds and cleanse their spirits, not to beat them with whips. Later, toward the end, he would repudiate violence with the unforgettable saying: "*All they that take the sword shall perish with the sword.*"

---

* Matthew, Mark and Luke place it later.

By his cleansing of the Temple, Jesus had committed an open act of defiance against the religious establishment of Israel. It was a grave offense, with political as well as religious significance. He had offended one of the most influential groups in the land, the Sadducees. These were the aristocrats of the Jewish community. They were a priestly order who felt themselves to be the appointed custodians of the Law of Moses. Rich and haughty, they disdained the common people and regarded the Temple as their special sphere of influence. They ran it as if it were a family business.

To the Sadducees, any attack on the Temple was an attack on the established order, a threat to the status quo —and to their profits and privileges. In their eyes, anyone who acted as Jesus did must be an enemy of society. The Sadducees were powerful, and their hostility could be dangerous.

How hazardous the open defiance of authority could be became apparent at this time with the arrest and imprisonment of John the Baptist. Like the prophets before him, John did not hesitate to expose immorality in high places. He had publicly denounced the governor, Herod Antipas, for putting aside his wife and taking his brother's in her place. According to the Jewish code this amounted to public adultery, and caused a great scandal in Palestine.

Antipas regarded the Baptist as a dangerous agitator, aside from his moral preachments. Many people were following him, and there was always the possibility that the Baptist might stir them up to the point of rebellion. So John was thrown into a dungeon in the desert fortress of Macherus to silence him once and for all. But this did not satisfy Herodias, the woman for whom Antipas had discarded his wife. She hated John and wanted him dead.

Her chance came when her daughter Salome performed an erotic dance for Antipas and his lords and captains at his birthday party. This sensuous exhibition so enthralled Antipas that as a reward he promised the girl anything she might fancy. Her mother urged her to ask for the head of John the Baptist. Even Antipas was shocked by the request but, bound by his promise, he complied. He had his executioners cut the Baptist's head off and presented it to Salome on a platter. *And the damsel gave it to her mother.*

(Curiously, Salome's name is never mentioned in the Gospel stories of the death of John. She is referred to only as *the daughter of Herodias.* We learn her name from the contemporary Jewish historian Flavius Josephus, not from the Bible. Scholars believe she was about thirteen or fourteen when she danced for Herod Antipas—the age when a Jewish girl would have been "most exciting to the carnal passions of men." She appears in only six or seven brief paragraphs in the New Testament, but Salome and her dance have repeatedly inflamed the imagination of poets, painters, writers and musicians: Oscar Wilde immortalized her in his sultry poem-drama *Salome;* Richard Strauss in his opera based on Wilde's work; Flaubert in his story *Herodias;* the artist Luini in a painting that hangs in the Louvre; and Hollywood, in more than one spectacular movie.)

The news of John's arrest and the hostility of the priests in Jerusalem prompted Jesus to return to his own country, to Galilee. He decided to make the return journey by way of Samaria. There he had a curious encounter with a woman at a well.

It was risky for a Jew to travel through Samaria. The province was wedged between Galilee on the north and

Judea on the south, and it was at odds with both places. The Samaritans hated the Jews on their borders, and the Jews detested the Samaritans as a low order of renegade and heathen.

The reason for the mutual hatred was, as usual in that part of the world, religious. The Samaritans did not regard Jerusalem as their holy city. They had broken away from the orthodox worship of Yahweh centuries before. They had set up a sanctuary of their own on Mount Gerizim, in their own province. This was sheer heresy, a mockery of the sacred Temple, and sufficient reason for every Jew to despise every Samaritan.

Jews who traveled in Samaria not only were liable to be insulted as they passed through, but also took the chance of physical attack. This made no difference to Jesus. It was indicative of how remote he was from the hatreds and prejudices of his time that, far from joining in the general condemnation of Samaritans, he made one of them the hero of one of his great parables.

What we know as the story of "The Good Samaritan" was told by Jesus as a lesson against bigotry and a plea for brotherhood. He taught that the love of one's neighbor comes next to the love of God in the scale of virtue. Once, when a listener asked him *"Who is my neighbor?,"* Jesus told the story of what happened to a certain man, a Jew, on the road from Jerusalem to Jericho.

This road, as his listeners knew, was infested by highwaymen and robbers. The man in the story was attacked and robbed. Stripped of his clothes, he was left for dead at the side of the road. It chanced that the first traveler to come along the road was a priest, a man from whom some sign of compassion might be expected. But the priest did not wish to become involved. He crossed over and continued on his way on the other side of the road.

Next came a Levite, a member of a clan traditionally

devoted to religious service. He took one look at the bleeding and unconscious victim of the robbers—and he, too, hurried on without stopping or helping.

But then a Samaritan came along the road, a member of a despised and hated people. He stopped and had compassion. He poured wine into the victim's wounds to cleanse them, and oil to soothe them. He bandaged the wounds, and lifted the man to the back of his donkey. He took him to the nearest inn and paid the host to take care of the injured man until he should recover.

Which of the three travelers, Jesus asked, was a neighbor to the victim of robbers? The answer was self-evident. And so was the lesson. Contrary to the current prejudice, it was the detested Samaritan who behaved most admirably. It was the Samaritan who demonstrated that any man in distress is every man's neighbor and entitled to the help of anyone in a position to give it.

So Jesus may have chosen the way through Samaria deliberately, even though there were other safer roads that would take him home to Nazareth. Perhaps he wanted to show that no land and no people were alien to him, and that the open heart knows no barriers or boundaries.

Crossing the boundary into Samaria with a few of his early disciples, Jesus paused to rest at a well near the town of Sychar, about twenty-five miles from Jerusalem. It was noon (*about the sixth hour*), when the sun was hottest, and Jesus was thirsty. While he waited at the well, his disciples went into the town to buy food for the midday meal.

As he sat alone, *there cometh a woman of Samaria to draw water* ...

It was not customary for a woman to come to the well at noon, and to come alone. Evening was the usual time, and then the women came in groups. This woman was evidently independent, if not bold. The presence of a strange man at the well did not deter her from coming to it alone. And Jesus was not reluctant to talk to a strange woman in a strange place, either. He asked her for a drink.

It may have been that his style of dress betrayed him as a Jew, but more likely the woman recognized him as a Galilean by his accent. She was startled that he spoke to her at all.

"*How is it,*" she wanted to know, "*that thou, being a Jew, ask a drink of me, which am a woman of Samaria? For the Jews have no dealings with Samaritans.*"

She knew that Jews were forbidden to drink from the same cups, or eat from the same plates, as Samaritans. What kind of Jew was this who chatted easily with a Samaritan woman and would even accept a drink from one?

Jesus may have been amused at the encounter. He answered in a rather teasing way, knowing she would not understand him but that her curiosity about him would be aroused. If she knew who it was asking her for a drink, he said, she would be the one making that request. Had she asked, he said, he would have given her a drink of *living water.*

Practical and hardheaded as women can so often be, she pointed out that the well was deep and that he had nothing to draw water out with—no bottle, no bucket, and no line to lower them with even if he had them. So how could he possibly give her a drink? Did he think he was greater than the patriarch Jacob, who once used this well himself, back in ancient times?

Instead of answering directly, Jesus became even more cryptic. Anybody who drinks my kind of water, he said, will never thirst again. It would be like a well of living water inside that gave eternal life to the drinker.

The woman was fascinated by this.

"*Sir, give me of this water,*" she begged. She would never again become thirsty or have to come back to the well with her waterpot.

She had understood nothing of what he meant. Jesus —perhaps teasingly again—abruptly changed the subject. He told her to go and get her husband and bring him back.

She said she had no husband.

He knew that. He also knew that she had had five husbands previously, and that the man she was now living with was not married to her. He told her so, and she was astonished at his knowledge of her.

"*Sir,*" she said, "*I perceive thou art a prophet.*" From then on she spoke to him with great respect, and if there was any note of banter in the previous conversation it vanished now.

The well was situated at the foot of Mount Gerizim, and she questioned him about the proper place to worship: in this mountain, the holy place of the Samaritans, or in Jerusalem, the holy place of the Jews?

The place of worship should make no difference, Jesus said. In his religion, place and ceremony would not matter. "*God is a spirit,*" he told the woman, "*and they that worship Him must worship Him in spirit and in truth.*" That was all that mattered.

Completely serious now, the woman said: "*I know that the Messiah cometh, which is called Christ. When he comes, he will tell us all things.*"

Now, considering the circumstances and the person he was addressing, Jesus made an amazing reply: "*I that speak unto thee am he.*"

It was his first acknowledgment to anyone that he was, indeed, the Messiah. Not to his family; not to his countrymen; not to his disciples: only to this foreign woman, a stranger—and a Samaritan!—did he make this supreme disclosure. And he made it to no one else so plainly again until shortly before his death.

Just at this point, as if on cue, his disciples returned. That ended the conversation, but it had an aftermath almost immediately.

The disciples, for their part, were greatly surprised to find Jesus talking freely and openly with an attractive woman. (She must have been attractive; how else could she have won five husbands and a lover?) Religious teachers were forbidden to converse with women in public or instruct them in private. Devout Jews would not even speak to their own wives on the street. Truly orthodox males quickly turned their faces to the nearest wall at the approach of a woman. But here at the well none of the disciples dared to say to Jesus, "*Why talkest thou with her?*" If Jesus did it, it must be right.

From the start, Jesus ignored and broke the primitive taboo that surrounded women in his society. Though no such term had been invented or heard of, he was a feminist. Over and over he showed by his speech and actions that he held women in the same regard and respect as men. He did not apply the double standard which said that sexual transgressions which were permitted to the male were inexcusable in the female. One of his most memorable encounters with the prejudices of his time involved a woman who was caught committing adultery, *in the very act.*

The penalty for this offense for a woman was stoning to death. The sinner was stripped half naked and her hands were tied behind her back. She was then taken to a high place and pushed off violently. If the fall did not kill her, stones were heaped on her until she was dead.

When the woman caught in the act was brought to Jesus, she was being used as a device to trap him. He was asked by churchmen what should be done with her. If he said that she should be stoned to death as the Law required, he would be passing a life-and-death judgment upon her. And this might bring him into conflict with the Romans, who did not decree death for adultery. On the other hand, if he simply absolved her, he would be going against the code of the Hebrews and, in effect, condoning the crime.

Instead of answering at once, *Jesus stooped down, and with his finger wrote on the ground, as though he heard not.* It is the only recorded instance of Jesus writing anything, and no one knows what it was that he wrote.

Then he stood up and replied to the churchmen who were pressing him for a judgment on the woman:

"He that is without sin among you, let him first cast a stone at her."

Again he stooped and wrote on the ground. When he looked up, he was alone with the woman. Her accusers had melted away.

"Woman," he said, *"where are they that accused thee? Hath no man condemned thee?"*

She answered: *"No man, Lord."*

And Jesus said: *"Neither do I condemn thee. Go, and sin no more."*

That was to be an episode in the future. But it was foreshadowed in the conversation with the woman at the well in Samaria.

Overwhelmed by her encounter with the mysterious stranger, the woman left and hurried into town, leaving her waterpot behind in her haste. She spread word of what the prophet had said to her—*"He told me all that I ever did"*—and the people of Sychar came to hear him. The woman of the well was his first apostle in Samaria.

For two days Jesus stayed there, preaching and teaching to the many who came to listen to him. Many believed in him, not because of what the woman had said about him but through the power of his own words and presence. It was an early demonstration of how he could project his teachings and himself upon his hearers, and make believers of them. *"This is indeed the Christ,"* said the people of Sychar. And they called him *"the Savior of the world"*—the world, they said, not just the Jews.

When he resumed his journey to Galilee he told his disciples to look at the fields of barley and wheat along the way. *"They are white and ready for the harvest,"* he said.

His own harvesting was about to begin.

Though Jesus would break radically with the past and teach the world a new doctrine, he chose an orthodox setting and a traditional way to proclaim the beginning of his public ministry. He chose the familiar synagogue in Nazareth as the place and a Sabbath service there as the occasion.

Perhaps in deference to his growing fame in the area, he was selected to read a passage from the Scriptures. Any male member of the congregation could be called on to perform this function in a synagogue service of the time. Jesus was given the "book" of Isaiah to read. It was not, of course, a book of the kind we know. It was a series of pieces of parchment, or vellum, sewed together in a long strip and attached to a roller at each end. The Hebrew characters were read from right to left, the parchment being wound from one roller to the other as the reading progressed.

What Jesus read at this Sabbath service was both a forecast and a summary of his mission:

> *The spirit of the Lord is upon me,*
> *because he hath anointed me to preach*
> *the gospel to the poor;*
> *he hath sent me to heal the brokenhearted,*
> *to preach deliverance to the captives,*
> *and recovering of sight to the blind,*
> *to set at liberty them that are bruised* ...

When he finished, he handed the book back to the attendant in charge of the service. *And the eyes of all them that were in the synagogue were fastened on him.* The words were the words of the prophet Isaiah, but Jesus clearly applied them to himself. *"This day,"* he said, *"is this Scripture fulfilled in your ears."*

At first his fellow Nazarenes seemed pleased and proud to have him as a teacher in their midst. They recognized him as Joseph's son, and Mary's, one of their own. But soon, almost at once, his message began to shock and offend them, as it would many others afterward. He was seized by an angry mob—what we would now call a lynch mob—and dragged from the town. He was taken up a high bluff, and pushed and hauled to the edge of it. They meant to hurl him down from it, and kill him.

He eluded them, and the home town of Jesus narrowly escaped the eternal disgrace of destroying him. All the world would come to know him as "Jesus of Nazareth," and he would be called "the Nazarene" ever afterward. But Nazareth rejected him and cast him out. He performed none of his major miracles and spoke none of his great sayings there. He was, as he himself said, without honor *in his own country, and among his own kin.*

After he announced his mission in Nazareth and was

rejected, he never lived there again. He shook the dust of the place from his feet, and made his way north to the town of Capernaum on the Sea of Galilee. This became his second home and the headquarters of his early ministry—"*his own city*," Matthew called it. He paid his Temple tax there and found his chief disciples in and around the city. The miracles and healings which the hostile atmosphere did not permit him to perform in Nazareth he did at Capernaum and near it.

There was trade in fish and fruit in Capernaum, and it was a center for collecting customs. There was a clattering bazaar, and a good deal of jostling and shoving in the narrow, cobbled streets which had to accommodate a population of some eighteen thousand. From a distance the place had a forbidding look, the houses and shops being built of basalt, a dark volcanic stone. Only the synagogue of limestone gleamed white and splendid in the sun. The population was mixed, Phoenicians mingling with Hebrews, and all under the eye of troops of the local Roman garrison.

But the chief significance of the place was that it was on the Sea of Galilee.

This was, strictly, not a sea at all, but a lake. It was only about thirteen miles long and eight miles wide, and could be crossed by boat in less than an hour. It was also known as the Sea of Tiberias and the Lake of Gennesaret, a word that may have meant "harp," which the lake faintly resembled in shape.

Small, as the waters of the world go, the Sea of Galilee looms large in the imagination of Western man because of its close and colorful connection with the story of Jesus. Without him it would be of no interest to any of us today that the sea, or lake, furnished a livelihood to many fishermen of the region, or that it was (and is) uncommonly lovely. It would not concern us that its waters sparkle blue and green in the sun, and are rimmed with oleander and mimosa and circled by verdant hills. As for the white and gleaming towns on its shores—Chorazin and Bethsaida and Magdala and Tiberias and Capernaum—we would never have heard of them.

But Jesus loved the Sea of Galilee. Much of his ministry unfolded along its shores or on it. The sea was subject to sudden and violent storms, and it was one of these that Jesus calmed with the words *"Peace, be still."* It was here that he astounded his disciples by walking on the water toward their boat (*about the fourth watch of the night*). Though carpentry was his trade, he spoke far more often the language of the sailor and fisherman. (*"When it is evening, ye say, 'It will be fair weather: for the sky is red' . . ."*) He was continually taking to ships and boats, sometimes to teach from them as listeners lined the shore, and sometimes to cross the lake on a journey (*. . . and he took ship, and came to the coasts of Magdala*).

On the water he found relief from the burden of his ministry and the demands of the crowds that pressed around him. (*But Jesus withdrew himself with his disciples to the sea . . .*) Once some Galilee fishermen worked all night and caught nothing until Jesus told them where to lower their net. Then their haul was so great that the net almost broke, and they took in enough fish to fill their own boat and another.

On the shore of Galilee he saw two men casting their nets into the water. They were brothers, Simon and Andrew. Jesus said to them: *"Follow me, and I will make you fishers of men."* Simon and Andrew left their nets to follow him and become his disciples.

He saw two other brothers, James and John, mending their nets in a boat with their father, whose name was Zebedee. He called to them also. Immediately, James and John left their ship and their father and followed him.

There was something compelling, something irresistible about him. It was a kind of authority that most men responded to eagerly, often without understanding what drew them on. A word, a look, was enough to persuade a man to break off his accustomed way of life, to drop what he was doing, and follow Jesus without question and without qualms for the future. It was not only rough-and-ready fishermen who obeyed instantly when Jesus said, "*Follow me.*" He saw a man named Matthew sitting at a table in the customs office at Capernaum, a clerk keeping a ledger and counting tax money. *And he rose and followed him.*

In this way he chose the men who would be his closest followers, his nearest disciples, the select number that would become known as the Twelve Apostles. All those he picked at this time were fellow Galileans—all except one. His name was Judas Iscariot, and he was from Judea.

The most fruitful period of the ministry of Jesus was confined to the region around the Sea of Galilee, and to four or five little towns that were all within a day's journey, or less, of each other. Because he walked and talked and taught there, this tiny segment of the earth outshines whole continents in its importance to mankind. During his brief ministry in this obscure and unlikely backwater of the world, Jesus made "an imprint on the human conscience which will last to eternity."

The quotation is not from some pious tract by a reverent churchman of the past. It is from a hardheaded twentieth-century tycoon named William Maxwell Aitken, better known to contemporary history as Lord Beaverbrook. One of England's most dynamic newspaper publishers, he also served as Minister of Information in the First World War and as Minister of Supply to Winston Churchill during World War II. As something of a genius of journalism, Beaverbrook was a master at winning and holding vast audiences by reaching the mind and stirring the emotions of the public. In this area he was an unequaled authority. Yet he called Jesus "the greatest propagandist the world has ever known."

"Propaganda" now has an odious sound, suggesting tricky methods of selling dubious ideas and spreading partisan lies. But in its original sense of teaching others to understand and accept new doctrines and ideals, Jesus was indeed a propagandist, and Lord Beaverbrook's tribute to him is accurate. Those who heard Jesus said of him: "*Never man spake like this man.*" And no one has spoken like him since.

He did the most radical and dangerous thing a prophet or preacher can do: He set about changing and reversing the morality of his time. People are shaken and societies tremble when long-established ideas of right and wrong are called into question, and when traditional concepts are challenged. Jesus boldly challenged some of the most ancient beliefs of his society, and the message he brought was unlike anything ever heard in the world before.

He went through every city and village, preaching and proclaiming the glad tidings of the kingdom of God. But the kingdom he spoke of was not, as many of his listeners hoped and believed, a visible and tangible domain that the Messiah would establish on earth to the trumpetings of angels and with pillars of fire. It would not be like that at all. When they asked him where and when it would come, he answered: "*Behold! The Kingdom of God is within you.*"

He said much that was new and strange and startling,

and what he said often contradicted what his listeners had been taught to believe for generations—for centuries. It was written in their Scriptures, in the Book of Exodus, that injury should always be paid back in kind: *eye for eye, tooth for tooth, burning for burning.* The Greeks and the Romans followed the same rule, which had seemed entirely reasonable to the whole human race from time out of mind.

Jesus rejected it.

He said: "*Whosoever shall strike thee on thy right cheek, turn to him the other also. . . . I say unto you: Love your enemies, bless them that curse you, do good to them that hate you . . .*"

It was an idea that went sublimely contrary to human nature and instinct. It was so revolutionary that it seemed —and still seems—absurd to many, if not to most. But Jesus knew that there was no other way to break the chain reaction of hatred and violence that has scourged the human race through all the centuries. Hatred inevitably generates hatred, and violence breeds violence. Blow for blow. Eye for eye. Death for death. Jesus proposed the only conceivable way out of the vicious circle in which mankind had trapped itself.

The dreams of most men in all times have been of wealth and the eminence that goes with it, but again Jesus went against the certainties of society. Over and over he denounced the pursuit of riches and exposed the spiritual corruption that so often accompanies affluence. "*Beware of covetousness,*" he warned, "*for a man's life does not consist in the abundance of the things he possesses.*"

The kingdom of God, he said, was open to all, but those who trusted in riches would find entry into it extremely difficult. His disciples were amazed at his vehemence on this point, but he told them: "*Life is more than meat and the body more than raiment.*" Materialism had the fatal flaw that what was gained by it was always threatened by losses that far outweighed it. *"What shall it profit a man,"* he asked, *"if he shall gain the whole world, and lose his own soul?"*

He preached the infinite value of the individual human being, an idea that astounded and enthralled his listeners. He taught the absolute equality of men and women before God, and he swept away with scorn the notion that rank and wealth had any bearing on the worth of a human being. God the Father cared for his children impartially, and they were all of equal value in his eye, even the humblest. No sparrow falls to the ground, said Jesus, without the Father knowing it. *"Fear ye not, therefore, ye are of more value than many sparrows."*

Jesus turned the values of the world inside out. Where the world admired power and envied wealth, he rejected both and gave their exact opposites his blessings. In his first recorded sermon—the "Sermon on the Mount"—it is the poor, the humble, the meek who are called "blessed" (happy or fortunate), not the rich and powerful and famous. *Blessed are the merciful,* not the mighty . . . *Blessed are the pure in heart,* not the clever and successful . . . *Blessed are the peacemakers,* not the warriors and conquerors.

He preached against greed and cruelty and self-righteousness, and always he stressed the power of love to purge the baseness from men and make them brothers. *"By this shall men know ye are my disciples,"* he said, *"if ye have love, one to another."*

It was a new teaching that he brought to the villages and towns of Galilee, a new religion that had nothing to do with formal creeds and set rituals. It required no altar, or priest, or Temple. His glad tidings of the kingdom of God had no need of slaughtered animals or money-changing. He lighted the way to a new path, a new time. *For the Law was given by Moses,* one of his disciples would write of him, *but grace and truth came by Jesus Christ.*

Between his journeys from town to town, Jesus stayed at the home of Simon the fisherman in Capernaum. Simon was a solid, hearty character who early won Jesus' approval and affection. Jesus gave him a nickname. He called him *Cephas,* or rock, which is translated as "Peter," and in the listings of the Twelve Apostles the name of Peter always comes first.

Once when Jesus was a guest in the house, Peter's mother-in-law was sick in bed with a fever, and Jesus was asked to do something about it. With another of those homey minor miracles, like the one in Cana, Jesus obliged. He touched the hand of Peter's mother-in-law, and the fever immediately left her. She got up out of bed and served dinner.

That Jesus could cure a serious fever with a mere touch of his hand was evidently taken for granted by all present. No special comment is recorded on the miracle, not even from the mother-in-law.

But Jesus was driven by a sense of urgency that did not allow him to enjoy rest and hospitality for long. *"Let us go into the next towns that I may preach there also,"* he would say. *"For therefore came I forth."* He was constantly under way along the dusty roads and shaded byways of Galilee. Sometimes he spoke in the open fields, sometimes on the shores of the lake, and sometimes from the side of a hill (a "mount") where his voice could carry over the crowd gathered below him.

He attracted crowds wherever he went—*much people,* according to one gospel, *great multitudes* according to another. Some of the people followed him about for days at a time, drinking in his sayings and unable to tear themselves away: *for his word was with power.*

It was not only what he said that drew the people.

There must have been something magically compelling about him as a person, some lure of voice and manner that those who saw and heard him found irresistible. He talked mostly to ordinary people—workmen, farmers, tradesmen, shepherds, housewives—and he spoke as one of them. He used plain, simple language. He drew illustrations from the workaday world his listeners were familiar with: the sowing of seed, a woman searching for a lost coin, a wedding feast to which nobody came, sheep that have strayed.

Not all of his sayings were new to those who heard them. Much of what he taught was familiar from the Scripture readings in the synagogues and from the wisdom of the rabbis, or teachers, handed down from generation to generation. Yet his way of saying what was familiar made it shine like something never heard before. And his way of revealing what was new and strange in his tidings was stunning. Some asked in amazement: *"What new doctrine is this?"* and *others wondered at the gracious words which proceeded out of his mouth.*

As his fame spread people thronged around him, not only from every part of Galilee, but from Judea and from Jerusalem, and from Decapolis and Perea, which lay on the other side of the Jordan to the south and east. People literally climbed trees to catch a glimpse of him. There was, for instance, Zaccheus the tax collector. He was short of stature and the press of people around Jesus blocked his view. So he climbed up a sycamore for a better look.

Passing by below, Jesus spotted Zaccheus in the tree, and called to him to come down. Then Jesus invited himself to the tax collector's home for dinner. Zaccheus was overjoyed, but some in the crowd were shocked. Tax collectors were not popular with the people, and eating with them was considered scandalous. But Jesus always ignored custom and convention when they interfered with his mission of fellowship and forgiveness.

Whenever word went around that he was in a certain place, people swarmed together to see and hear him. Stopping at Peter's house another time, he found himself besieged by a crowd so dense that no room was left inside and the doorway was blocked by the throng outside. Four men came carrying a paralyzed friend on a litter, but they could not get inside the house. In their desperation to bring the sick man to Jesus, they hoisted the litter over the heads of the crowd to the roof. There they took up some of the tiles and made a hole big enough to lower the litter down by ropes into the room where Jesus was. He astonished everyone present by curing the man of his paralysis on the spot. The crowds that followed him everywhere increased.

Even without the miracles, his personality exerted a power that is now called "charisma"—the power to attract and hold followers, and to move them to wonder and homage. Today we know the gracious words that fell from his lips, and they still retain their original beauty and wisdom. But concerning the person of Jesus himself, the physical man capable of inspiring such love and adoration, we know nothing at all.

There is no existing evidence, written or visual, on whether he was tall or short, slim or heavy, handsome or plain. In all the four Gospels—in the entire New Testament—there is not a word of physical description of him. Everyone is free to make his own mental picture of what the human Jesus looked like, since no actual picture of him exists or ever existed. The thousands and thousands of paintings and drawings of him, some by the greatest artists who ever lived, are sheer guesswork.

The Jews had a commandment in their Book of Exodus that prohibited making a likeness of anything, whether human or animal or inanimate. This was an outgrowth of the Jewish abhorrence of idolatry, the fear of being tempted to bow down and worship statues and images as the pagans did. So no sketch, and certainly no finished portrait, was ever made of Jesus while he lived. The taboo against making any likeness held for several centuries after his death, even among his non-Jewish followers, the early Christians. By the time the first pictures of Christ were made, no reliable memory of what he looked like survived. The first artists, like all the succeeding ones, had to rely on their imaginations.

Over the centuries, artistic imagination has produced a wild variation of images of Jesus. Early pictures were scratched on the walls of the catacombs, the caves in Rome where Christians took refuge from their persecutors. They showed him as young and beardless. In the art of the Eastern Empire, after the fall of Rome, the Byzantine artists pictured him quite differently. They showed him as fierce and forceful, sometimes even ugly. Several hundred years passed before Western art evolved the prevailing image of him as sweetly handsome, with delicate, classic features and soft, compassionate eyes. A similarity of image gradually developed. With one artist following the lead of the preceding one, a more or less standard picture of Jesus was established.

This familiar and accepted portrait is highly idealized, and cannot be anywhere near correct. Jesus spent much of his life outdoors in a semitropical country where the sun usually beat down hot and bright. His complexion would have been tanned and dark, if not leathery. Swarthy complexions are the rule in Mediterranean countries now, and it would have been no different in Jesus' time.

Having been a manual worker, and probably a builder used to handling heavy materials, he was no doubt well developed physically. The attack on the money-changers was a display of vigor and virility. His constant travels afoot up and down the rugged terrain of Palestine indicate that his energy was formidable and his stamina great. Energy and stamina are not usually associated with the kind of gentle, subdued personality pictured in so many of the classic paintings.

On the other hand, he was not necessarily a brawny stevedore type, either. He may well have been handsome and graceful of movement and gesture, since being strong and active does not imply being crude and clumsy. The women of Nazareth and Magdala were famous for their beauty, and it is seldom that a region produces lovely women and ugly men. The probability is that Jesus looked pretty much like the other men of his time and locality, with no obvious physical features to set him apart. At the time of his betrayal, Judas had to kiss him to identify him for the arresting soldiers. Otherwise they would not have been able to pick him out from the men around him.

He very probably had a beard and long hair parted in the middle, like most Jewish men of his time. The Romans were clean-shaven and wore their hair short, so beards and long hair were signs of defiance and resistance among the Jews, even if their own tradition did prescribe the style as well. But hair and beard would have been well groomed and tidy, since unkempt hair was frowned on. So was hair that was excessively long, which was called a shame to a man but a glory to a woman.

His clothing, like that of the men around him, would have been a linen tunic that came a little below the knees.

(The loose, billowing robes that reached to the ground, as shown in religious paintings, would have been highly impractical in hiking through the dust of Palestine and climbing in and out of fishing boats.) In cooler weather a woolen cloak would be added, and from this tassels dyed deep blue dangled at the hem. The tassels were yet another of those everyday reminders of a man's relation to God and His commandments. A napkin-like arrangement, a kind of kerchief, covered the head with ends falling down over the neck. This not only protected against the sun and absorbed sweat, but also in Jesus' case was a gesture to propriety. No Jewish teacher would appear in public with his head uncovered. On his feet would be simple sandals consisting of a flat sole of leather bound to the foot and ankles by thongs.

In spreading the gospel from village to town, and pausing to preach on the plains and hills as they went, Jesus and his disciples led a strenuous, headlong life. Their style of living was simple and close to the earth, geared to a minimum of wants and a total lack of luxuries.

The lake gave them fish, the trees supplied fruits, and in the bushes were blackberries. Dates and figs were everywhere, and so were olives. Meat was largely reserved for special occasions like wedding feasts, and so was wine. Wherever they went they could rely on the hospitality even of strangers, for the custom of the land required it. When it was necessary to buy something, the money was taken from the common purse. Judas had been chosen to hold the purse and manage the money.

If there was no shelter nearby when night fell, they wrapped themselves in their cloaks and slept on the ground in the olive groves and under the fig trees. So mobile and unsettled was their way of life that Jesus himself warned of its hardships when men volunteered to join him. The foxes have their holes to rest in, he said, and the birds of the air have their nests. But he, Jesus, had no place of his own to lay his head.

His demands on those who would follow him were stern and uncompromising. One man who signified a willingness to join him asked if he could bury his father first. Jesus said to him: *"Follow me. Let the dead bury their dead."* Most of the apostles were married, but Jesus did not allow their family relationships to interfere with their mission. His own family life, too, had ended when his ministry began. After the wedding at Cana, no domestic encounter with his mother is recorded. The physical strain of following him, and the emotional demands it made upon them, caused some of the disciples to drop out from the group and go home.

For those who remained, including the Twelve who were closest to him, Jesus remained a mystery and an enigma. They were mostly rough, earthy men and they sensed that he was of a different order of being from themselves. Some of what he said was beyond their ability to grasp (. . . *they understood not his saying, and were afraid to ask him*). The range and contrast of his moods often surprised and baffled them.

He could be cool and reasonable—shrewd, in fact—and he could rise to mystical heights where they could not follow. He could be sweetly indulgent and forgiving to the humble sinner, but terrible in his wrath against hypocrites and exploiters. He seemed always conscious of the presence of God and of his relationship to God, yet he could submerge himself in the everyday concerns of those around him, and participate in the life of the least of his followers.

Still, he was never entirely one of them. There was always something reserved and withheld about him. *He knew what was in man*, what men were like.

In the give and take of daily contact on the road and elsewhere, the disciples and Jesus dealt with each other on strictly human terms. Once, on the way to Capernaum, he heard several of his followers quarreling among themselves as they walked along the road. When they reached the house, Jesus asked them what the dispute was about. He was curious.

But they wouldn't tell him.

Actually, they had been arguing about who was to rank the highest among them, a favorite topic of speculation in the group. On another occasion, the mother of James and John came to Jesus and asked him to give her sons preference in his forthcoming kingdom. She thought that one of her boys ought to be chosen to sit on his right hand and the other on his left.

Sometimes, when he said things they did not want to hear, they *rebuked* him—and he rebuked them back. Sometimes they became impatient with him and heckled him about his promises and prophecies. They pressed him for straight answers: *"Tell us, when shall these things be?"* Their obtuseness could exasperate him into exclaiming, almost in despair, *"How is it that you do not understand?"* They were capable of such lapses as embarking on a voyage and forgetting to take any food along.

On the other hand, the strain of constant travel afoot, managing Jesus' tours through Galilee, and coping with the crowds that continually swarmed around him was enough to tax the strength of even the hardiest fisherman. Sometimes, it is recorded, *they had no leisure to so much as eat.*

His disciples were often more protective than Jesus liked. Once a group of mothers brought their children to him to receive his blessing, and the disciples tried to prevent them. They scolded the mothers for bothering Jesus when he was tired after a long day of walking and teaching. But Jesus, seeing what was happening, was displeased with what his disciples were doing. He told them to stop it.

"*Let the little children come to me,*" he said. "*Do not forbid them. For of such is the kingdom of heaven.*" The children gathered around him and he laid his hands on them in the gesture that meant blessing among the Jews.

Jesus turned to his disciples and said: "*Verily, whoever shall not receive the kingdom of God as a little child, shall not enter into it.*"

To accept his doctrine of love and forgiveness, to find the way to God and a new life, required the openness and innocence of a child. "*Become as little children,*" he taught, and God will receive you as his own. Throughout his ministry he showed unending gentleness and compassion for the young and weak, while his harshness was reserved for the powerful and cruel.

But his disciples were right. He did grow weary and discouraged, and he needed rest. Whenever he could he withdrew himself from the suffocation of the crowd, from the strain of public appearance and teaching, from the quarreling and questioning of his followers. He would send the crowds away and go up a mountain alone, to be by himself. Or he would go to a solitary place in the desert to pray. Often he would get into the boat of one of his fisherman disciples and put off from shore to find solitude on the sea. Sometimes he awoke early in the morning before anyone else was up, and found an isolated spot for prayer and meditation.

His disciples would go looking for him and bring him back, perhaps scolding him a little for running off. Everybody, they said, was asking for him ("*All men seek for thee*"), and the crowds would gather around him again, and he would be moved by compassion for them. He would begin to teach again.

It was on such an occasion that he performed one of his most famous miracles, the only one described in all four Gospels:

A great multitude had followed him into a plain near the city of Bethsaida, and he began talking to them of the kingdom of God. He and his listeners became so absorbed in what he was saying that the day wore away and the sun began to set. His disciples became uneasy. Here was a huge crowd out on an open plain, with no provisions for supper and no way of getting food. The disciples urged Jesus to send everybody away to forage for victuals as best they could.

There were five thousand men, women and children to be fed, and Jesus asked his disciple Philip how this was to be done under the circumstances. Jesus asked the question only to test (tease?) Philip, *for he knew himself what he would do*. Philip had no idea of how to solve the problem. He pointed out that the company's purse contained nowhere near enough money to buy food for so large a crowd.

Then the disciple Andrew made what he thought was a hopeless suggestion. *"There is a lad here,"* he said, *"who has five barley loaves and two small fishes. But what are they among so many?"*

We are not told the name of the remarkable boy who seems to have been the only one foresighted enough to bring along something to eat. But Jesus took his loaves and fishes and blessed them, looking to heaven as he did so. He then gave the skimpy store of food to his disciples. He told them to distribute it among the people, who were now sitting on the grass in groups of hundreds and fifties. As the loaves and fishes were passed around through the crowd from hand to hand and mouth to mouth, the miracle happened.

The supply of bread and fish did not diminish.

When everybody had eaten his fill, Jesus instructed his disciples to gather up all the leftover fragments of food—*"that nothing be lost,"* he said. The leftovers from the five loaves and two small fishes filled twelve baskets.

Such miracles increased his fame and swelled the crowds that milled around him, and he began to be hailed as a prophet everywhere. Until now he had been spreading his teaching through Galilee in the manner of other rabbis, or teachers, *and the common people heard him gladly.* He had made no open claim to divinity, judging the time not yet ripe. But those around him were increasingly aware that Jesus, for all his human traits and behavior, was more than human.

He often referred to himself as the *Son of Man,* which is a literal translation of the Aramaic phrase meaning "human being" or "the man." But as Jesus used it of himself (and nobody else applied the term to him) it had a special significance, a more mystical one. It indicated his humanity as an equal counterpart to the divinity implied by the other title given him: *Son of God.* He knew that this duality in his nature was a mystery difficult, if not impossible, for the people around him to grasp—as it has been for his followers ever since.

At a place called Caesarea Philippi he once asked his disciples: *"Whom do men say I am?"* They told him that some said he was another John the Baptist, while others believed him to be Elijah or Jeremiah or some other ancient prophet come back to life.

Then Jesus asked another question: *"But whom say ye that I am?"*

Peter spoke up for himself and for the rest of the disciples: *"Thou art the Christ, the Son of the living God."*

This was the first open declaration by any of the Apostles that the man they were following was, indeed, the long-awaited Messiah. The prophet for whom they had left their boats and nets and families was the Christ, which was not a name but a description and a title—*christos*, meaning the Anointed One, the one appointed to be the Savior.

Jesus seemed greatly pleased by Peter's answer and called him *blessed* for making it. What Peter said showed Jesus that the men closest to him understood who he was and what his mission in the world was to be. As if reassured that his disciples were now capable of facing what was to come, Jesus from then on began to prepare them for the agony and death that awaited him.

The times were turbulent, rebellion was in the air, and Roman authority was constantly alert to any sign of possible sedition. But Jesus and his band were able to move freely from place to place without arrest or interference. The Romans could be bloodily ruthless when they felt the interests of their empire to be menaced. But as long as civil order was maintained and taxes paid, they were not inclined to meddle into the internal affairs of the people they ruled over.

Their attitude toward the customs and beliefs of the Jews was one of contemptuous indifference. Zealots, or anyone who attacked the state, would be run down and exterminated. But the authorities saw little harm in preachers wandering about and spreading their crackpot religious doctrines here, there, and everywhere. Roaming preachers and itinerant fanatics were no novelty in Palestine, and Jesus seemed to be just another of the breed. The Romans did not suspect even dimly that, in the long run,

Jesus and his teachings were a greater threat to their empire than any resistance movement or any number of enemy soldiers.

The danger to Jesus came from another quarter.

It came, as he told his disciples, from men called *elders, chief priests and scribes*—from what we would call the intellectuals, the established order, the defenders of tradition and the past. It came from those who sneered "*Out of Galilee ariseth no prophet*" when others were hailing him as the Redeemer.

So there was a division among the people because of him. . . .

Sometimes the sound of a trumpet attracted the attention of passersby on a street in Jerusalem, usually in the vicinity of the Temple. When people turned to see what was happening, they would find themselves spectators at a little show staged for their benefit: A man with fringes on his robe would be making a public display of giving alms to a beggar.

On a street in Jericho a man might be standing with his face raised to heaven and praying in a loud voice. He would pretend to be unaware of people passing by, but he would make sure they could hear him. He would thank God that he was not like other men, but more righteous, just and pious than they.

Or in a crowd in Capernaum another man might attract attention to himself by turning his head abruptly to the nearest wall at the approach of a woman. He would not allow his eyes to rest on her, and he wished everyone to notice that he was avoiding the very sight of a female.

All three would be wearing robes with ritual fringes that were longer than customary dangling from the hems. They would also be wearing phylacteries strapped to their foreheads and left arms. These amulets, or charms, were tiny leather boxes containing passages from Scripture. They, too, would be larger than usual to make a more impressive show of the wearer's piety.

All three men would be Pharisees.

They were members of a guild, or society, which considered itself the supreme guardian of the sacred traditions of the Jews. There were about six thousand of them, and some were rabbis and some were laymen. But all of them looked upon themselves as defenders of the spiritual purity of Israel against contamination from within and without. They insisted on the strictest observance of the Law and of tradition. They set themselves up as shining examples of how good Jews should conduct themselves before God and their fellow men.

Some Pharisees were, in fact, sincere in their faith and deeply devout. The great Rabbi Hillel was one of them, and there were other influential teachers among them. But, along with the Sadducees, they dominated the religious life of Israel, and with power came a corrupting pride. For many Pharisees the spirit of the Law and the moral richness of Jewish tradition were smothered in the routine of ritual. The show of piety meant more to them than its substance.

Israel regarded itself as a theocracy, a state ruled by God rather than by any secular or civil authority. Religion determined law, custom and tradition, which gave organizations like the Pharisees and the Sadducees extraordinary influence. Aligned with them were the priests of the Temple, the magistrates known as *elders*, and the Scribes.

The Scribes were originally responsible for making

accurate copies of the Scriptures, but in time became teachers and interpreters as well. They functioned as lawyers and judges in religious courts, and were a power in their own right.

It was this array of entrenched authority that Jesus came up against when he went about preaching his new doctrine, spreading his revolutionary sayings, and setting aside the traditions and taboos of centuries. A conflict was inevitable.

With the increasing fame of Jesus in Galilee, travelers brought news of him and his ministry south to Jerusalem. There the authorities were disturbed by what they were told of this new prophet who had arisen among the people. They determined to check on him and his activities, and sent some of their own people north to observe, take note, and report back. The authorities then, as now, had their undercover agents.

The agents were shocked at what they found.

"*How is it,*" they asked the disciples in amazement, "*that he eateth with publicans and sinners?*"

This was a serious charge. It was guilt by association. Decent men did not sit down at table with sinners, and certainly not with publicans.

Publicans were minor tax officials. They were Jews who collected taxes from other Jews and turned the money over to the Roman government. They were hated and despised as traitors, and treated like criminals. And here was Jesus visiting their homes and dining with them, as he did with Zaccheus who climbed the tree to see him. Not only that, but one of his own disciples—Levi, later known as Matthew—was a publican!

Jesus' reply to the charge that he was outraging public decency by such actions was simple: His mission, he said, was to bring the kingdom of God to those who needed his tidings most—to the outcasts of society. Healthy people, he said, do not need a physician. The sick do. It was not the righteous man who needed his ministry. It was the sinner.

Jesus' disciples, being earthy, hearty men, did not always observe all the rules and regulations prescribed by the priests and Pharisees. Sometimes they ate without washing their hands first, and they were not finicky about the cleanliness of the pots and pans they used, either. This, too, was a grave offense. The orthodox code set great store by ritual washing and cleansing. The Scribes from Jerusalem were horrified again.

But when they reproached Jesus, he was far from apologizing. Instead, he responded with heat and made his own accusations against them. He charged them with being hypocrites who quibbled over the surface formalities of religion while ignoring its essence. Their talk about men being "defiled" if every detail of the dietary laws was not observed was nonsense, he said. *"There is nothing from outside a man that, entering into him, can defile him,"* Jesus told them. *"But the things which come out of him, those are things that defile a man."*

It was this bold disregard of old and sacred rules that aroused the hostility of the Pharisees and Scribes and priests. It was his habit of stripping away the surface sham and insisting on the essence of things that they could not, and would not, tolerate.

They used what we now call "smear" tactics against him, accusing him of being *a glutton and a winebibber*, a drunkard, because he sometimes attended feasts and banquets. To the Pharisees he was a rank outsider, an upstart who had no credentials as a teacher and who belonged to no recognized school or sect. His teachings were therefore not only suspect, but also dangerous. Scribes and priests were angry when they found themselves the targets of his parables and when he called them *the blind leading the blind*. They were furious when he taught that *publicans and harlots* would *go into the kingdom of God* before hypocrites such as they.

They were continually trying to trick him into saying something damaging that would cause him trouble with the Roman authorities or turn his own followers against him. As with the woman caught in adultery, they would demand answers of him in controversial situations, hoping to *entangle him in his talk* or *catch something out of his mouth, that they might accuse him.*

Though the Gospels tell of Jesus weeping, they never describe him as laughing or even smiling. Many of his sayings show, however, that he had a sharp wit and a dry, ironic humor. Repeatedly he defeated hostile questioners with a crisp retort—what we would call a "topper"—and sent them away in confusion with a line for which they had no reply.

Once, hoping to turn the political situation against him, they came with a loaded question they were sure would entrap him. They began by flattering him. They called him "Master" and praised him as a great teacher. Then they asked him: *"Is it lawful for us to give tribute unto Caesar, or not?"*

This was a burning question in Israel.

For people who regarded God as their only authority, the payment of tribute, or taxes, to a foreign ruler was particularly galling. It was not only a financial imposition, to many Jews it seemed a religious outrage as well. And that was the two-way snare that had been set for Jesus.

If he answered that the levy should not be paid, his reply would instantly be reported to the Roman authorities and he would be subject to arrest for sedition. But if he should answer that the tax was just and should be paid without question, he would offend the Jews and turn the people against him.

Jesus immediately understood the craftiness of the question, and he knew how to counter it. He asked to be shown a coin of the kind used for paying taxes. (He evidently had no such money on him.)

They brought him a Roman penny, and he held it up for all to see. The head of the Emperor Tiberius was engraved on it, with his title.

"*Whose image and description is this?*" Jesus asked them.

"*Caesar's,*" they answered.

One can imagine Jesus flipping the coin back to its owner with a shrug as he said:

"*Give unto Caesar, therefore, the things which are Caesar's—and unto God the things that are God's.*"

Even his questioners, we are told, were forced to marvel at the cleverness of his answer. They could not *take hold of his words*. Unable to think of anything to say, they went away in silence, leaving Jesus unscathed in another encounter that was meant to destroy him.

Losing such verbal skirmishes naturally increased the hostility of the Scribes and Pharisees against him, but what sent shock waves through their ranks was something more serious. Everywhere he went, Jesus exercised a special power which astonished the people, won him hundreds of converts, and alarmed the religious establishment. It was the power to heal.

. . . they brought unto him all sick people that were taken with different diseases and torments, those which were possessed of devils, and those which were lunatic, and those that had the palsy; and he healed them.

One such healing marked for Jesus a decisive break with the past and put him in danger of his life. It occurred in

Jerusalem at a place called Bethesda, near the Sheep Market. There was a pool at Bethesda whose waters were supposed to work wonders. It was believed that at certain times an angel passed over the pool and ruffled the surface of the water.

According to tradition, the first person to enter the pool after the waters were disturbed would be cured of whatever ailed him. There were five terraces around the pool, and they were always crowded with the sick and crippled waiting their chance to be first into the water after the angel came.

Jesus noticed one of the cripples, a man who had been waiting at Bethesda for thirty-eight years. The man explained to Jesus that he had no one to put him into the pool. Somebody always got in ahead of him because he couldn't move fast enough by himself.

Jesus took pity on him, and said, *"Rise, take up thy bed, and walk."*

Instantly the man's infirmity left him. He stood, picked up the pallet, or mat, he had been lying on for so many years, and walked away a well man.

Now a curious difficulty developed. Instead of being congratulated by everyone on his miraculous cure, the man was denounced for walking about carrying his bed. It was a Sabbath day, which, according to the code of the Pharisees, made it unlawful for anyone to do any kind of work. Carrying one's bed was work.

The recovered cripple defended himself by saying that he had been told to do so by the man who had cured him.

What man had done this?

A man called Jesus.

Jesus, in turn, was sought out and charged with breaking the Sabbath, which in Israel was not only a religious offense, but a crime.

Sabbath observance was precious to the Jews because

it was so particularly their own. Other sects and religions also had temples and scriptures, but they did not have a Sabbath. So every good Jew was expected to conform without question to the many restrictions which tradition had imposed on the day.

Something like twelve hundred ordinary actions, according to one estimate, were forbidden on the Sabbath. Many of the rules were petty and arbitrary, and had no real relation to the worship of God. For instance, it was forbidden to eat an egg laid on the Sabbath because the hen had worked to lay it. A stick could not be dragged along the ground because that might be regarded as plowing. And so on.

Jesus ignored these meaningless restraints. To him it seemed absurd that God would be offended by having a good deed, such as the healing of a cripple, performed on His day. He answered his accusers by saying that since his heavenly Father never ceased His work, neither would he.

This infuriated the Pharisees even more. Now they raged against him not only because he had broken the Sabbath, but because he had also put himself on a level with God. Now they wanted not merely to punish Jesus, but to kill him.

Another time, on another Sabbath, he cured a man who was born blind. Jesus spat on the ground, made a little dab of clay, and rubbed it on the man's eyes. When it was washed off, the man could see. This miracle caused particular amazement because, as the people said, *since the world began it was not heard that any man opened the eyes of one that was born blind.* A man who could do that, the people said, must be from God, else how could he bring about so marvelous a thing?

But again the Pharisees were unmoved by the miracle. They were only outraged by another violation of their code. This man, they said, could not possibly be from

God because he did not keep the Sabbath. It was yet another black count against Jesus in the indictment they were compiling against him.

But Jesus went his way, insisting that *"the Sabbath was made for man, not man for the Sabbath."* His liberal and liberating attitude on this issue became one of the chief causes of contention between him and the religious leaders of Israel.

The miracles he performed disturbed many, not only the priests and Pharisees. People were *astonished beyond measure*, but not all the reaction was favorable. Some who saw him cure terrible diseases like leprosy with a touch, or make a madman sane with a word, were seized with fear. A crowd that witnessed one of his more spectacular healings turned on him and drove him away. He had to take ship to escape their anger.

His miracles have been a source of dispute and controversy ever since. People still ask, as they did then: *"How can these things be?"*

Reports of miracles were common in the time of Jesus. The idea that God, or the gods, could intervene in human affairs and tamper with the laws of nature in doing so was accepted everywhere. Jesus himself certainly believed in miracles and in his power to perform them. Over and over he stressed the element of faith in his healings. If the victim believed sincerely that Jesus could heal him, then he would be healed: *". . . all things are possible to him that believeth,"* he said.

Science itself now tells us that the power exerted by the mind can sometimes change the condition of the body. Today we know something about "psychosomatic" illness, where physical distress is caused by mental disturbance. With the proper mental adjustment, the bodily illness disappears. Some such principle, it can be argued, was in operation in Jesus' cures. The power of his personality, the force of his mind, overcame the emotional maladjustments of those whom he healed.

Reports of similar cures are common enough in our own time. Millions of people believe that miraculous recoveries occur at the Catholic shrine at Lourdes or at emotionally charged revival meetings conducted by faith healers. Christian Science literature regularly reports a wide range of afflictions that have been cured by the power of mind over matter. A respected American reporter in India in the 1970s writes a book about a holy man known as "Baba." Multitudes of Indians accept the holy man as an incarnation of God. "Baba works miracles practically all day, every day," says the reporter. "Baba heals. He makes objects appear from nowhere. He reads the past and sees into the future."

In short, what the Gospels ask us to believe happened in Galilee two thousand years ago is not so wildly different from what millions of people are ready enough to believe today.

Our own marvels—radio, television, atomic energy, trips to the moon—would seem utterly incredible to the people of Jesus' time. They would find it far easier to believe that a holy man could cure a leper, or that a prophet could walk on water, than to accept the idea of men flying around the world five miles up in the air, or sitting at home and watching what was happening thousands of miles away.

What one age finds totally unbelievable another age takes for granted.

Still, there is clearly a supernatural element in the miracles attributed to Jesus. They cannot be explained or made to seem rational by glib parallels and modern analogies. They can only be accepted or rejected. Believing Christians accept them on the basis that the Almighty who made the universe could suspend or alter the laws of that universe to suit His own purposes. Believers simply accept the saying of Jesus: *"With God all things are possible."* Others may regard the miracles as part of the myth-making that surrounds all the truly towering figures of the human past.

The survival of Jesus in the imagination of mankind has not depended on whether or not the stories of the miracles ascribed to him are literally true or only symbolic. In all ages past, there have been plentiful reports of wonder-workers and magicians whose feats caused astonishment and awe in their time. But the world no longer takes them seriously, or even remembers them.

Jesus is remembered.

But in "smiling Galilee" the clouds began to gather around him. The joyous reception of his early teaching gave way to mistrust, anger and fear. Hundreds whom he had won over remained his faithful followers, but there were many who turned against him.

Some were bitter that he had not preached the overthrow of Rome and the coming glory of a Jewish state. For them his "kingdom of God" was too remote and nebulous. Many were put off by the uncompromising demands of his doctrine, which required a selflessness that seemed impossible to achieve.

Once a young man came to ask him how to inherit eternal life. Jesus told him: Keep the Ten Commandments, love God, and love your neighbor as you love yourself. "I do all that," said the young man, "and always have." Jesus looked at him and added one more requirement: *"Go and sell whatever you have and give to the poor,"* he said. By doing so the young man would himself become poor but would gain for himself treasures in heaven. "*Then*," said Jesus, "*come and follow me.*"

The young man, who was rich, went away. His possessions meant more to him than the prospect of eternal life that Christ had offered him.

There were others who were bewildered and confused by his astonishing words and deeds. They thought he must be possessed by a devil, which was the current explanation for behavior that was regarded as wildly unconventional or improper. Even those closest to Jesus, his friends and relatives, sometimes tried to protect him from hostile action by explaining that he was mentally unbalanced. "*He is beside himself,*" they said.

Even the places he loved best, the towns around the Sea of Galilee, often seemed cold to his teachings. It drove him to despair and anger. *He grieved for the hardness of their hearts*—the deadness of heart that would not respond to his message of love and repentance. He promised them a life more rich and free if his teaching was followed. "*I am come that they might have life, and that they might have it more abundantly,*" was one of his sayings.

But they would not listen.

It moved him to grieve for the cities which, like his own Nazareth, rejected him. He lamented for Chorazin and Bethsaida, and for his adopted home of Capernaum, too. Sodom itself would have survived, he said, if the mighty works had been done there that he had performed in Capernaum. But Capernaum had turned its back. Like the wicked city of Sodom in the Old Testament, it too was doomed to destruction. The prophecy came true. Today no one any longer knows for sure the original site of Capernaum.

But his ministry in Galilee was far from a complete failure. The word had been spoken, many had heard it, and many believed. One of his parables, those little stories he told to illustrate his points, applied to his efforts in Galilee.

He told of a man who set out to sow seed across his acres. Some of the seed fell by the wayside, and the birds ate it. Some fell on stony ground, and some was choked by thorns. But much of the seed that the man scattered abroad fell on good ground. In time it brought forth its fruit, some of it a hundred times over. So it was, he said, with the word of the kingdom. The seed had been planted. It would grow and spread beyond what anybody then alive could imagine.

Galilee, he knew, was not the place for the appointed climax of his earthly mission. For a Jewish prophet, there was only one place for that. *"It cannot be,"* he said, *"that a prophet should perish outside of Jerusalem."*

Ever since Peter's avowal of his divinity at Caesarea Philippi, Jesus had been preparing his disciples for what was to come. *"We will go to Jerusalem,"* he would say to them, *"and the Son of Man will be betrayed to the chief priests and Scribes, and they shall condemn him to death...."* He foresaw it all: the scourging, and the mockery, and the crucifixion. He told them of the great mystery to come as well: *"And on the third day he shall rise again."*

The disciples understood none of it, and were afraid to ask him what it all meant. But they followed him when he left Galilee, being by now deeply involved in his mission and closely attached to his person.

A group of women also went with him.

They were as closely attached to him as the men and, as events would show, even more faithful to him. Among them was Mary of Magdala, known as Mary Magdalene, whom he had cured of a severe emotional disturbance (*seven devils had been cast out of her*). Another woman who followed him was Joanna, the wife of one of Herod's officers. There was one known only as Susanna, and there were many others whose names are no longer known. These women *ministered to him of their substance*—from their own resources they provided for the day-to-day needs of Jesus and his disciples.

Neither the disciples nor the women knew that when they left Galilee they were embarking on a Via Dolorosa, a way of sorrow.

But Jesus knew.

The long walk south to Jerusalem, by way of Jericho, was a final journey.

It was the way to Golgotha.

IT WAS FALL, when September fades into October, *and the Jews' Feast of Tabernacles was at hand.*

This was also called the Festival of Booths, and it was a time of rejoicing. The harvest was in, the barns and bins were bursting with fruit and grain, and the vats were brimming with wine and oil. It was a time of thanksgiving.

For the Jew it was more.

This was a great religious festival as well. It lasted eight days, and it recalled the time when the children of Israel wandered in the desert for forty years after being delivered from slavery in the land of Egypt.

In memory of the tents they lived in then, the Jews now built booths, or huts, out of myrtle branches and palm leaves. They built them around the Temple and in all open spaces—on their flat roof tops, in their gardens, in squares and courts. All through the festival the Jews lived not in their houses, but in the green and fragrant booths.

Jerusalem took on a holiday look. People carried around bundles of reeds and willows tied with bright ribbon as symbols of the festival. They exchanged presents and chanted *"Hallelujah, Glory to God!"* as the ritual required. In the Temple many animals were sacrificed, and at night thousands of huge torches blazed up against the dark.

In the midst of this celebration and rejoicing, Jesus came to Jerusalem. As a practicing Jew, he too participated in the feast. He, too, lived in one of the improvised green booths, or tabernacles. His was on the Mount of Olives, just outside the city with a view toward the Temple. It was a favorite spot of his.

He had not been in Jerusalem for eighteen months, but many people recognized him. The stories of his miracles had spread, and his cure of the crippled man at the Bethesda pool was remembered. Every day when he went to the Temple people gathered around to hear him speak and listen to his teaching.

In Galilee it had been comparatively safe for him to preach his doctrine freely. There people were inclined to be more receptive to what was new and different. In Judea the atmosphere was sterner and harsher, like the land itself. Here there was less tolerance and more insistence on the old ways and on the ancient faith, more fanaticism. And here Jesus was under the direct scrutiny of the officials of the Temple itself—the priests, the Pharisees, the Sadducees.

Here in Jerusalem he was at the very core of the concentrated power of Israel. Now no word or act of his would go unnoticed or unrecorded by those who wished him ill and could cause him harm. *They feared him, because all the people were astonished at his doctrine.*

Nevertheless, he now spoke more openly and daringly than ever before.

Previously, throughout his ministry in Galilee, he had been restrained—almost secretive—about his Messiahship and his divinity. Even when he received Peter's acknowledgment at Caesarea Philippi he had urged his disciples that they should *tell no man that he was Jesus the Christ.*

But now he spoke of himself in a high, exalted strain that left his listeners in no doubt. *"I am the light of the world,"* he said. *"He that followeth me shall not walk in darkness, but shall have the light of life."*

And he said: *"I am the way, the truth, and the life: no man cometh unto the Father but by me."*

And again: *". . . I proceeded forth and came from God. Neither came I of myself, but He sent me."*

These were sayings that put him on dangerous ground with many devout Jews, not only with priests and Pharisees. For many, such words had the awful ring of blasphemy, an affront to God. He seemed to be putting himself on a level with Yahweh, an intolerable idea to orthodox Jews. On one occasion Jesus did just that without qualification:

"I and my Father are one," he said.

This was too much for many of his listeners. They would have fallen upon him and stoned him to death, but, as before, he escaped from their grasp, and this time retired to the country beyond the Jordan, *where John at first baptized*, and remained there for a while. Even in that barren place people sought him out, and he taught them.

Though his teachings were mostly of love and compassion and the enrichment of the spirit, he also spoke of damnation. There would come a day of judgment, he said. Those who rejected the Kingdom of God would be called upon when the world ended to account for how they had spent their lives. There would be a hell, *a furnace of fire*, for sinners.

Whether this was meant literally or figuratively, Jesus did not stress the idea of hell or of sin. "Sin" was a word that was not often on his lips. He had demonstrated repeatedly that he did not regard the violation of man-made edicts and invented ritual as sinful in itself. Sin for him consisted in the corruption of the spirit that made the love of God and of one's neighbor impossible. It meant cruelty, oppression, and the meanness and hatred that poison life at its roots. He demanded in human beings a purity of spirit like his own—a purity that could be achieved only by believing in him and his teachings, and following his way.

In his furious denunciations of the Scribes and Pharisees, the most damaging word he used against them—and he used it over and over—was: *hypocrites!* Because they used piety and pretense as a cloak for spiritual corruption, he called them *a generation of vipers*, an assemblage of poisonous snakes. For robbing widows and exploiting the poor while at the same time intoning long prayers in the Temple, he compared them to whitewashed tombs—"*which indeed appear beautiful on the outside, but within are full of dead men's bones, and all uncleanliness.*"

Self-righteousness that masked an inward evil, the show of virtue that covered greed and avarice, these were sins in the eyes of Jesus. They caused him to cry *woe! woe! woe!* upon the religious leaders of his time, and to ask them: "*How can ye escape the damnation of hell?*"

While Jesus was still in temporary retirement on the River Jordan, he received an urgent message from two dear friends of his, sisters named Mary and Martha. They sent him word that their brother Lazarus, whom Jesus also loved, was gravely ill.

They urged Jesus to come at once.

Mary and Martha lived in a town called Bethany, which was a little less than two miles from Jerusalem. By the time Jesus reached it, Lazarus had died. Martha came out a little way from Bethany to meet Jesus, and the first thing she did was scold him for not getting there in time. *"Lord,"* she said, *"if thou hadst been here, my brother had not died."*

Like others close to Jesus, Martha regarded him as human enough to be subject to reproach, just as any other friend might be; but she was also sure that, in some way she did not understand, he possessed superhuman powers.

Jesus assured her that her brother would rise again, and she believed him when he comforted her with a saying that has been repeated many thousands of times since:

"I am the resurrection and the life: he that believeth in me, though he were dead, yet shall he live.

"And whosoever liveth and believeth in me shall never die."

Martha went off to tell her sister that Jesus had come. All three went to the grave of Lazarus, which was in a cave with a large rock closing the entrance. As they stood there—the two sorrowing sisters with their friend—

Jesus wept.

It is the shortest verse in the Bible (John 11:35). In two words it says much of the simple humanity that Jesus shared with Mary and Martha, and with us.

There were other mourners present, relatives and friends of Lazarus. Jesus asked that the stone be moved from the entrance of the cave. Martha, who was the practical sister, objected. *"Lord,"* she said, *"by this time he stinketh."* Her brother had been dead four days.

Jesus reassured her. If she believed strongly enough, he said, she would see with her own eyes evidence of what he called the *glory of God*.

The stone was removed, and Jesus said in a loud voice: *"Lazarus, come forth."*

The man who had been dead came out from the cave and into the sunlight. He was still wrapped in the linen bindings in which he had been put into his grave.

"Loose him, and let him go," said Jesus. . . .

It was not the first time, the Gospels tell us, that Jesus had shown his mastery over death.

Once, in the town of Nain in Galilee, he had come upon a funeral procession. A young man, the only son of a widowed mother, was being carried to his grave. Moved to pity by the weeping mother, Jesus touched the bier as it passed. The procession stopped.

Jesus spoke: *"Arise!"*

At once the young man sat up, and Jesus returned him alive to his mother.

There was, too, the daughter of Jairus, an official in a synagogue. The girl was only twelve years old and she was dead when Jesus arrived at her house in response to the father's plea. A crowd of mourners was there wailing and lamenting, but Jesus told them the girl was not really dead. She was only sleeping. If her father had faith enough, all would yet be well.

The mourners knew better. They scoffed at Jesus—*laughed him to scorn.* He ordered them from the house.

Then he took the girl by the hand as she lay pale and motionless, and said to her in Aramaic: *"Talitha cumi."*

We can imagine him saying it softly and gently, as the mother and father looked on in breathless anxiety and suspense—"Get up, little girl." Immediately she got to her feet and began walking around.

The story ends with one of those lovely little touches in the Gospels where something awesome and incredible is made warm and believable by an utterly human detail. Once the little girl was miraculously brought back alive and well from her journey into death, Jesus *commanded that something be given her to eat.*

The raising of the widow's son at Nain and of Jairus' daughter had both taken place in Galilee—out in the sticks, as we would say. The reports that reached Jerusalem could be dismissed as old wives' tales from the hinterland where people would believe anything.

But with Lazarus it was different.

This was a miracle reported to the priests and Pharisees by eyewitnesses fresh from the scene. A man had been raised from the dead, not among gullible peasants in faraway Galilee, but in the very shadow of the Temple itself.

Priests, Pharisees and Sadducees gathered in a council and asked each other: "What shall we do about this man?" His miracles were causing excited talk in the streets and were winning new followers for him every day. His teachings were turning devout Jews away from the ancient Scriptures and leading them to think in new and unorthodox ways. If this continued, the whole social system of Israel would be undermined. The prestige and also the profits and privileges of the rulers would be threatened. And all this because of an upstart from Nazareth who had no fixed address, no steady occupation, and no credentials as either a teacher or a preacher. From the viewpoint of the rulers it was an intolerable situation.

The decision of the council was that Jesus must die.

So instructions were issued that anyone who knew of Jesus' whereabouts and could identify him for the authorities should report to the council. His arrest would be ordered at once.

Aware of the ominous atmosphere in Jerusalem and not yet ready to give himself up, Jesus lingered with his disciples at a place called Ephraim, some distance north of the capital. But the great feast of the Passover was approaching again and Jesus, like the good Jew he was, made ready to go to Jerusalem to observe it. For all his boldness in defying the empty conventions of the past, he continued to observe the spirit of the Law. He had come, he said, not to destroy the Law but to fulfill it.

On his way to Jerusalem for what he knew would be his final visit, he stopped off again at Bethany. There a supper was prepared for his honor, with Martha as usual serving the meal. Lazarus was also among those present. Many people were milling through the town because word of Jesus' coming had spread. The crowd also wanted to catch a glimpse of Lazarus, the man who had come back from the grave. He had, in fact, become such a curiosity that the priests now intended to have him killed too, because he was visible evidence of the supernatural powers of Jesus. The raising of Lazarus had caused too many Jews to believe that the man from Galilee was, indeed, the promised Messiah.

During the supper, Mary crouched at the feet of Jesus and broke open a small jar made of alabaster, a creamy-white stone that resembled marble. She poured the contents of the jar over Jesus' feet. It was a fragrant and costly oil called spikenard. Mary bathed Jesus' feet in it, and then wiped them with her long hair as the sweet smell of the oil filled the house.

It was a warm and impulsive gesture from a warm and impulsive woman to a friend she deeply admired and loved. But the fragrance of the oil was still in the air when one of the disciples spoke up to condemn Mary for what she had done.

The oil, he said, was worth every bit of 300 denarii

(about $60), which was a great deal of money indeed. It was enough to pay a laborer for a year. Why had Mary wasted it so foolishly? It could have been sold and the money given to the poor.

But Jesus had appreciated Mary's gesture, and now he defended her: "*Let her alone,*" he said. She had done a good thing, and her deed would be remembered for all time wherever the Gospel was preached. The poor would always be there but he, Jesus, would not.

The disciple who had objected was silenced.

His name was Judas.

He was usually called Judas Iscariot because he came from Kerioth, which was a town in the south of Judea. He was the only one of the Twelve who was not from Galilee, and this must have made him something of an outsider in the group. Now he was about to make himself an outsider and an outcast of the whole human race.

The Gospel tells us almost nothing about him. He was the "son of Simon," but who this Simon was we never learn. We do know that Judas was the treasurer of the Twelve and *had the bag,* or purse. His fellow disciple John records that he was a thief, and presumably stole money from the common funds of the group. We do not know how the other disciples felt about him before he committed his crime, but Jesus, speaking to the Twelve, once said: "... *one of you is a devil.*" He meant Judas Iscariot.

Perhaps Judas had been brooding for a long time over what he intended to do, and the rebuke he received at Bethany was only the last of the grievances that stirred him into action. He went straight to the chief priests and told them that he was ready to betray Jesus to them.

"*What will ye give me, if I deliver him to you?*"

The priests were glad to see him, and probably did not haggle over the price. They agreed on thirty pieces of silver (about $30). *And from that time Judas sought opportunity to betray him.*

It seems unlikely that money—so paltry a sum!—was his only motive. But if it was not, why did he agree to do so infamous a thing?

Nobody knows.

Perhaps he had joined Jesus in good faith, seeing him at first as a prophet in the ancient tradition of the Jews. But then he may have become alarmed at the increasingly radical tone of Jesus' teaching. He saw the new doctrine as a threat to the whole structure of Jewish law and tradition, and he felt it his duty to act before it was too late.

Another theory is that he sincerely believed Jesus to be the Messiah and only meant to hasten the coming of a new order in Israel by turning Jesus over to the authorities. Jesus, he hoped, would then be forced to assert his power, destroy his enemies, and assume his rightful place as ruler of the world.

But it has also been suggested that Judas was a spy for the priests and Pharisees, and intended to destroy Jesus and his movement from the start by boring from within, as undercover agents still do today.

There is no evidence for any of these theories. As one scholar has said, "Judas is, and will remain to the end of time, a mystery of evil." Luke's explanation for what motivated him will have to suffice: ". . . *Satan entered into Judas*. . . ."

Jesus and his disciples, now numbering only eleven, took the Jericho road that led to Jerusalem. The road was alive with pilgrims on their way to celebrate the great feast of the Passover in the Holy City. Many of them were Galileans who recognized Jesus, and his presence added to the excitement that every pilgrimage to Jerusalem brought with it. It was spring, the month of Nisan, which is our April. Budding greenery and bird song accompanied the wayfarers as they surged along the curving road that bent around the Mount of Olives as it neared Jerusalem.

A shout went up when the first view of the city, with its golden Temple gleaming in the sun, burst upon the eyes of the pilgrims. Suddenly spread before them was the place called Zion—*the city of our God*, as the psalm sang of it, *the joy of the whole earth.* For a devout Jew, there was no sight like it in the world.

But for Jesus the dazzling scene was clouded by his awareness of what was about to happen to him there. Looming up behind the Temple was the Tower of Antonia, which represented the power of Rome. It dominated the city and everyone in it. Between the Temple and the Tower, the authority of Israel and the might of Rome, his fate would be decided.

First, though, there was a moment of triumph.

His disciples obtained an ass for him, one of the long-eared beasts that did all-around hauling and carrying service in Palestine, where horses were a rarity. But a donkey was also a symbol of lowliness and peace. No man riding one could possibly be mistaken for a conquering hero.

The disciples threw their cloaks over the donkey, making a kind of saddle for Jesus to sit on. Mounted on this unlovely animal Jesus rode into Jerusalem—but he did not enter unnoticed.

Enthusiastic crowds surrounded him every step of the way. Many of those who cheered and saluted him were the pilgrims from Galilee, but there were others who were wildly excited by his coming as well. The whole city was in an uproar, and when people asked, *"Who is this?"* they were told: *"This is Jesus the prophet of Nazareth of Galilee."*

This was the prophet who raised Lazarus from the dead, and preached so stirringly in the Temple, and taught a new doctrine to the people.

Men cut down branches from the trees and laid them in his path, and others spread their garments on the ground for Jesus' donkey to walk over. They came waving palm leaves to greet him. It was a Sunday—the day that would be known thereafter as Palm Sunday.

And the people shouted *"Hosanna!"* which was like saying, "God save the king!" *"Hosanna in the highest,"* they cried. *"Blessed is the King of Israel that cometh in the name of the Lord!"*

There was no mistaking it: to the shouting thousands of Jerusalem the humble man astride the plodding donkey was the Messiah, come at last....

But for the priests and Pharisees, the reception given Jesus was a storm warning. *"Behold,"* they said to one another, *"the world has gone after him."* They were losing control. Jesus was winning over the people. Action against him could not be long delayed.

As for Jesus, he was not misled by the popular acclaim. His purpose could not be accomplished by cheers and shouting in the street. He told another of his parables to illustrate the meaning of what was about to happen. A grain of wheat, he said, is nothing by itself. Only when it falls into the ground and dies does it bring forth its richness, its fruit.

His coming ordeal was much on his mind, and he spoke of it repeatedly in different ways, sometimes plainly and sometimes obscurely. He told his disciples what the larger meaning of death would be: *he would give his life as a ransom for many.* His death would not be a mere martyrdom. It would be a sacrifice for the whole world. "I am the good shepherd," he said. *"The good shepherd giveth his life for his sheep."* A single saying that would one day be called "the Gospel in a nutshell" summed up his mission on earth:

"For God so loved the world that he gave his only begotten son, that whosoever believeth in him should not perish, but have everlasting life."

It was a doctrine that enthralled his followers but only hardened the determination of the religious establishment to silence him. A special session of the Great Sanhedrin was called in the palace of the High Priest, whose name was Caiaphas. Jesus was pronounced an outlaw.

The Sanhedrin was a council of seventy-one priests, scribes, and elders who exercised both civil and religious authority from which there was no appeal. On all matters of faith and conduct that affected the people of Israel, the Sanhedrin was both Senate and Supreme Court.

But the business of seizing Jesus would have to be conducted with great caution. The city was in an explosive mood. The popularity of Jesus had been all too clearly shown by the public demonstration at his arrival in Jerusalem. The authorities would have to proceed guardedly, *lest there be an uproar among the people.*

Jesus himself went about teaching in the courts of the Temple as before, making no effort to conceal himself. As the day of the feast approached, his disciples asked him what preparations they should make for the traditional Passover supper. None of them, including Jesus, had a home or house in Jerusalem where they could go for the celebration.

Jesus directed his disciples to a certain address in the city where, he said, a certain man would be found who would provide accommodations for them. This turned out to be true. The man was where Jesus said he would be, and he made available *a large upper room furnished and prepared.* It was Thursday, and that night Jesus and the Twelve met together there. Judas had rejoined the group.

The meal began at sundown, which was the start of a new day for the Jews. This was in accordance with the Scripture story of the creation of the world: *And the evening and the morning were the first day.* For the supper in preparation for the Passover, the hour of sundown was announced by blasts from silver trumpets throughout the city.

In the upper room there was one of the usual wrangles among the disciples as to who should have the place of honor nearest to Jesus. To rebuke them, and to show how little regard he himself had for rank and position, he took a basin of water and a towel and washed the feet of all the disciples. He did it over their protests, as a lesson to them. If he, their master, could stoop to do that, they for their part could show the same humility toward each other. *"I have given you an example, that you should do as I have done to you,"* he said. (To this day the Pope in Rome, during Holy Week, washes the feet of twelve poor men in memory of Jesus' act at the Last Supper.)

The meal itself was prepared and eaten in the way that tradition required. Four ritual cups of red wine were passed around, and passages from the Psalms were recited. The meat was roast lamb, as it had been centuries before at the first Passover. The bread was unleavened, made without yeast as the Scriptures demanded. Plates of bitter herbs were placed around the table. The herbs were dipped in dishes of sauce and eaten with the bread and meat.

The food was taken with the fingers, and Jesus and the disciples reclined on low couches, or divans, as they ate.

They rested on their left sides, with the right hand free to eat with from the low tables.

The Passover was usually a joyous feast, but the heart of Jesus was heavy. The mood of the whole gathering became grave when he announced that seated at the table with him was the man who would betray him. In alarm and dismay, the disciples asked him, one after the other: "Is it I?"

Judas also asked: "*Master, is it I?*"

Then said Jesus unto him, "*What thou doest, do quickly.*"

Judas got up from the table, left the room, and went out into the night.

The others did not understand what was happening. They thought that Judas, as treasurer, had gone off to carry out some errand that Jesus had given him. They would surely have stopped him had they known what he was about to do.

In these last hours with his disciples—he called them his "little children" and his "friends"—Jesus spoke to them with unusual tenderness. He spoke of how he must leave them soon, but he also gave them a sweet assurance: "*Let not your heart be troubled . . . ,*" he said. "*I go to prepare a place for you.*" In the intimacy and warmth of his last conversation with his friends in the upper room, he talked repeatedly of his love for them and of the love he wished them to have for each other. He spoke unforgettably:

"*A new commandment I give unto you: That ye love one another as I have loved you. . . .*"

He said this to them in several ways that night, as if to stress it as the heart of his teaching. And in a reference to the event that he knew lay just ahead, he also said:

"*Greater love hath no man than this, that a man lay down his life for his friends.*"

In the course of the meal Jesus introduced a ceremony, a rite, which Christians have been observing ever since as the greatest of their sacraments. He instituted the Sacrament of the Eucharist.

He took a piece of bread, gave thanks, and broke it in pieces which he passed to his disciples.

"This is my body which is given for you," he said. *"This do in remembrance of me."*

Then he passed around a cup of wine, saying:

"This cup is the new testament of my blood, which is shed for you."

With those few words Jesus formulated one of the great mysteries of Christian belief: Holy Communion.

Through all the centuries since, Christians have debated the interpretation of his words that night in the upper room. Did he mean that when the rite was repeated afterward by his followers, the commonplace bread and wine would miraculously be transformed into his true body and blood? Catholics believe this. At the communion rail they actually eat the body of God and drink His blood. Other Christian denominations think differently.

To many the Eucharist is an act of commemoration, a ceremony that reverently recalls the Last Supper and the meaning of Christ's sacrifice. *"This do in remembrance of me."* The bread remains bread and the wine remains wine.

But whatever view is taken of it, the Eucharist is one of the earliest sacraments of the Christian church, and it remains one of the most solemn and moving. Through the rite of Holy Communion tens of millions of men and women have felt that they have come closer to Christ. They have "communicated" with him, and with God.

That night in the upper room when the meal was over and his discourse finished, Jesus said: *"The hour has come...."*

He and the disciples sang a hymn together, and went out into the night. They walked eastward, toward the Mount of Olives. It was dark now, and the unlighted streets of the city were deserted. One of the disciples, Simon Peter, was carrying a sword under his cloak. Judea was infested with robbers and cutthroats, and the streets of Jerusalem were not always safe by night.

As they walked along, Jesus made another of those statements that so often surprised and upset his disciples. Before the night was out, he said, all of them would desert him. What would happen was already written in the Scriptures, and he quoted: "The shepherd will be struck, and the sheep will scatter."

All of them protested. None of them would desert him, they insisted, not one. Peter was especially vehement. "Lord," he said, "*I am ready to go with thee, both into prison and to death.*"

Jesus replied with another prediction: That very night, he said, Peter would deny him, betray him, three times before the rooster crowed twice.

Once outside the walls of the city, they crossed the brook Kidron and walked along a ravine, while a full Passover moon shone whitely on the olive trees. When they reached the west slope of the Mount, they climbed up toward a garden that was a favorite spot of Jesus.

The garden was called Gethsemane.

Here Jesus' mood grew downcast and depressed. "*My soul,*" he told his disciples, "*is exceeding sorrowful, even unto death.*" He asked them to keep watch while he withdrew to be by himself. When he was alone, he fell on his knees and prayed.

Now came the episode known to Christians as the "agony in the garden." During it, one Gospel records, Jesus literally sweat blood in great drops that fell to the ground. "*O my father,*" he pleaded, "*if it be possible, let this cup pass from me."* In Biblical language a "cup" that had to be drunk stood for anguish, terror and death. But after he pleaded to be spared the ordeal he was facing, Jesus added: *"Nevertheless, not my will, but thine be done."*

In the Garden of Gethsemane, the mystery of the dual nature of Jesus was demonstrated with special intensity. Without shedding his divine attributes, as Christians believe, he retained his full human nature and suffered the most extreme terrors of mind and spirit. His divine self knew that he must drink the full cup in order to fulfill the ordained plan for the redemption of the world. But his human self recoiled in panic and dread at the suffering he knew would have to be endured.

Three times, in his agony, he broke off his prayers to come to where his disciples were—*about a stone's cast away.* Each time he found them asleep. At first he was hurt, and he gently chided Peter: "What, couldn't you stay awake and keep watch for a little hour, as I asked you to?" But the last time, when he found them asleep again, he was resigned. It was late; they were tired; *their eyes were heavy.*

So, with perhaps a sympathetic shrug or smile, he said: *"Sleep on, now. Take your rest...."*

Judas, when he left the upper room, had made up his mind that the time had come for him to act. At supper Jesus clearly showed that he knew what was in Judas' mind, so now there was no time to lose if the compact for the thirty pieces of silver was to be kept.

As one of the Twelve, Judas knew the habits and customs of the group. He knew of Jesus' fondness for the Mount of Olives and for the Garden of Gethsemane. There may even have been talk among the disciples at supper that they would be spending the night in the garden after the meal.

Judas went to the chief priests and told them that he knew where Jesus could be found that very night. He offered to lead the way himself.

The priests reacted promptly. They assembled the Temple guard, a force of officers and men that was always at their disposal. With the mood of the city so unsettled, and with riot and uprising in the air, the Temple police were reinforced by soldiers of the Roman garrison. Should the attempt to arrest Jesus cause resistance that the Temple troops could not suppress, the Romans would intervene.

Anything could happen at Passover time, with Jerusalem packed full of pilgrims keyed up religiously and patriotically, which for the Jews was the same thing.

The troops came to the Garden with torches and lanterns blazing, even though the moon was bright enough that night. They did not know whether they might have to go searching for Jesus in caves or deep among the olive groves. They came, too, with weapons. Some carried clubs and some carried swords.

Jesus was speaking with his disciples, now awake, when the soldiers arrived. The soldiers did not know which one in the shadowy group that confronted them was the man they were looking for. Judas offered to make the identification. *"The man I shall kiss,"* he said, *"that is he. Take him, and lead him away...."*

Judas then went up to Jesus and greeted him with the salutation that was due a rabbi or teacher: *"Hail, Master!"* And he kissed him.

The Temple soldiers immediately stepped forward and seized Jesus, putting him under arrest.

It was too much for Simon called Peter when they laid hands on his beloved Master. Impetuous as always, he reached under his cloak and drew his sword. Then he slashed out at one of the soldiers, a member of the Temple guard named Malchus. Peter's wild blow missed its mark. It glanced off Malchus' head, but in doing so it cut off his right ear.

Jesus was shocked at this outburst of armed violence from one of his own disciples. He told Peter to put away his sword. Didn't Peter know that if Jesus wished it, his Father would instantly send legions of angels to protect him? But the ordained plan of sacrifice and redemption must be carried out. It was here, to impetuous Peter, that Jesus spoke his words about those who take the sword: *they shall perish with the sword.*

Then Jesus touched the bleeding wound at the side of Malchus' head and made his ear whole again.

If the arresting soldiers were impressed by this sudden miracle performed before their eyes for the benefit of one of their own, they gave no evidence of it. Perhaps it only confirmed what their priests had told them: they were dealing with an outlandish and heretical character who deserved to be put away in the interests of good order and public tranquillity. They bound his hands and led him away.

The soldiers took him back across the brook Kidron and into the dark and ominous city. There they brought him to the residence of the most powerful man in Israel, the former High Priest, whose name was Annas. For nine years this shrewd and domineering Sadducee had ruled the Temple. Even now the reigning High Priest, who was called Caiaphas, was his son-in-law.

It appears that Annas and Caiaphas lived close by each other in separate residences connected by a central courtyard. This was an arrangement common in the East. During the night Jesus was hauled back and forth between these two powerful men and interrogated like a common criminal.

Ordinarily, the laws of Israel were strict in trying a man for any important crime. Only the Jews, among all the nations of the time, rejected the testimony of informers in court cases. The corroboration of at least two witnesses was required before an accused man could be convicted. No one could be condemned to death on his own testimony—the same legal safeguard that is embodied in the Fifth Amendment of our own Constitution.

But emotion was running so high against Jesus among the rulers of Israel that many of these restraints were disregarded when he was brought to judgment. The priests and elders feared that the whole structure of their society was being assaulted by this outsider and his revolutionary doctrines. Men are seldom scrupulous when their basic beliefs and economic supports are being threatened.

There was another factor that added to the headlong urgency with which the case against Jesus was pressed by his prosecutors. He was arrested on the eve of the Passover, and his case would have to be disposed of before the Holy Day officially began on Friday at sundown. Once it did, all such activity as interrogation and trial would have to be suspended.

There was no one to stand by Jesus now. He was alone. His disciples had all forsaken him.

Perhaps, as good Jews, they were intimidated by the awesome authority of the High Priest, the only man on earth permitted to enter the Holy of Holies and come into the presence of Yahweh Himself. And, as they had seen in the garden, the High Priest's spiritual authority was backed by the arms of the Temple guard and of the Romans as well. Then, too, Christ himself had taught them not to resist, hadn't he? So they all melted away into the night.

All but one.

Peter followed at a distance when Jesus was taken away by the soldiers. His overpowering anxiety as to the fate of Jesus drew him on when the others fled. He came into the courtyard of the High Priest and unobtrusively joined a group of servants there.

It was evidently a chilly spring night, for there was a fire going and Peter edged up to warm himself at it. One of the serving girls began to look at him intently. Then she said to the group: *"This man was also with him."*

Somebody else in the circle backed her up, repeating the charge. Peter denied it hotly.

"Man," he said, *"I know not what thou sayest."*

Nearby a rooster crowed.

Around the fire they kept pressing Peter, ignoring his denial. Another girl pointed out that his accent betrayed him as a Galilean. Everybody knew that Jesus was one, too. The connection was clear.

But Peter denied it again.

Then one of the men in the group came forward to say that he was related to Malchus, the soldier whose ear Peter had cut off. "I was in the garden when it happened," this man said. "Didn't I see you there?"

For the third time Peter denied it.

And immediately the cock crew.

Just then Jesus appeared in the courtyard, as he was being led to another confrontation with his accusers. He heard Peter's denial. He heard the cock crow. He said nothing.

St. Luke, in his Gospel, merely writes:
And the Lord turned, and looked upon Peter.
The look was enough.
Peter went out and wept bitterly.

When morning came, Jesus was brought before the Great Sanhedrin in full assembly. It was presided over by Caiaphas, who had already expressed the opinion privately that Jesus ought to be executed. That, said Caiaphas, would be the best solution to the unrest that this disturber was causing among the people. Better that one man die than that the whole nation should be thrown into turmoil and possibly destroyed as a result.

With Caiaphas presiding, the verdict of the Great Sanhedrin was a foregone conclusion.

Jesus was face to face with the men he had openly denounced as "whitewashed tombs"—*whited sepulchers*—full of dead men's bones and all uncleanliness. The Sanhedrin was dominated by Sadducees, whose profits from the Temple were endangered when Jesus drove out the money-changers. In addition, the Sadducees did not believe in life after death. Before them was a man who had made a mockery of their doctrine by bringing the dead back from the grave.

They tried without success to bring false witnesses against him. They tried to make him out to be the leader of a dangerous underground movement. But he replied, "*I spoke openly to the world. . . . In secret I have said nothing.*" They could not deny it.

They referred to him contemptuously as "*this fellow . . .*" and accused him of threatening to destroy the Temple, a terrible crime if it could be proved against him. But Jesus' words were deliberately misquoted. He had spoken of destroying "this temple" and in three days building it up again, but he meant the temple of his own body.

Sometimes he stood mute and answered nothing to their accusations. When he gave answers that his questioners did not like, he was struck and spat upon, an unheard of outrage in a court of Israel. The soldiers would strike him from behind and mock him, saying, "You're a prophet. Prophesy who hit you!"

The climax came when Caiaphas, in all the solemnity of his high office, asked Jesus: "*I adjure thee by the living God that thou tell us whether thou be the Christ, the Son of God.*"

It was the crucial question on which everything else would depend.

Jesus answered: "*I am.*"

It was his first statement, openly and to the world, that he was indeed the Messiah.

When the High Priest heard the words of Jesus, he rose to his feet and began to tear at his clothes. To rend, to rip one's garments was the ritual reaction for any Jew who heard a blasphemy being uttered. It was a sign of horror and protest at being present when anyone dared to insult the great God Jehovah for whom anything but the humblest adoration was unthinkable.

Other members of the Sanhedrin also signified their indignation by tearing their clothes, which could never be worn again afterward. Now there was no further need of witnesses or questioning. For Caiaphas and the Scribes and Pharisees the issue was settled. The trial of Jesus was over. He had not only proclaimed himself to be the Messiah, which was intolerable enough. Worse, he had claimed to be *the Son of God*, thereby making himself godlike and divine. This was shocking beyond all reason

—and it provided the pretext the Sanhedrin was looking for.
They all condemned him to be guilty of death.

With seventy-one members of the Sanhedrin participating, the verdict passed on Jesus could not long be kept secret. News of it spread, and among the first to hear it was Judas Iscariot.

He had, apparently, been lurking near the Hall of Hewn Stone where the Sanhedrin met. There he accosted some of the priests and elders as they emerged from the meeting. By now, for reasons we do not know, Judas had *repented himself* and was overcome with remorse at what he had done. He tried to give back the thirty pieces of silver, thrusting them upon one of the priests as he said: *"I have betrayed the innocent blood"*—"I have caused the death of an innocent man."

The priests swept past him with contempt. "What's that to us?" they answered him. "It's your affair. . . ."

They walked on by.

Judas rushed to the Temple and flung the thirty silver pieces inside the doorway. Then he went away, found a barren place, and hanged himself.

Even then something ugly and disgusting happened to him. The rope on which he dangled from the limb of a high tree on the side of a cliff evidently broke. The record says that he fell headlong and *burst apart in the middle, and all his bowels gushed out.*

At the Temple, meanwhile, the thirty pieces of silver had been gathered up, and there was a debate among the priests about them. It was blood money, they decided, and so could not properly be put into the Temple treasury. What to do with it? The priests decided, finally, to use the money to buy a potter's field, a common cemetery to bury strangers and drifters in.

The place was named *The Field of Blood*, and is still known as that today.

By one of those coincidences that keep occurring in history, a new Roman governor had arrived in Judea at almost the same time as Jesus began his public ministry.

The name of this governor, or procurator, was Pontius Pilate.

If this proud Roman could have known how future generations would regard him, he would have been astounded to learn that he was to be remembered for one reason only: because his name was once linked with that of the Jewish agitator called Jesus of Nazareth. As Anatole France suggested in his famous story "The Procurator of Judea," Pilate could probably not even recall the name of Jesus after his brief contact with him. For Pontius Pilate, the man from Galilee would be just another administrative problem, one among many, to be forgotten as soon as it was disposed of.

Pilate had been an army officer, a regimental commander, which meant that he was a no-nonsense Roman used to giving orders and used to being obeyed. He must have been particularly tough and two-fisted; otherwise he would not have been assigned to Judea, which was one of the most unruly provinces in the whole Empire.

Almost as soon as he took office Pontius Pilate antagonized the people he was sent to rule over. When his troops marched into Jerusalem they were carrying standards and banners with images on them—the imperial eagles and pictures of the Emperor Tiberius. This outraged the Jews. Their laws sternly prohibited such images, because they resembled the idols which the pagans worshiped. In Israel there was no worse abomination than idolatry.

When the Jews staged a mass protest, Pilate had his soldiers infiltrate the crowd in disguise. Then he announced that the protestors would all be slaughtered on the spot if they did not disband immediately and go home. Instead, the Jews threw themselves on the ground and bared their necks to the Roman swords. They would rather die than submit to having their sacred Law violated.

Pilate was forced to back down. He ordered the offending standards and banners withdrawn from Jerusalem.

He caused another riot when he took money from the Temple treasury to build an aqueduct that increased Jerusalem's water supply. This was a badly needed public work, and anywhere else would have been welcomed by the people. But the Jews resented it furiously. No Roman had the right to touch money that belonged to their holy Temple, for whatever purpose.

So in Judea there was contempt on the part of the governor for the people, and hatred on the part of the people for their governor. They lived together in a state of mutual wariness and tension.

There was not much contact between them. Pontius Pilate was seldom in Jerusalem. He spent his time in Caesarea, a city much more to his taste. It was on the Mediterranean coast, and it had some of the magnificence of the great Roman cities. It boasted a hippodrome for chariot and horse races, and an amphitheater, or stadium, that seated twenty thousand for gladiatorial games and athletic contests. Lofty towers, visible to ships from afar, rimmed the beautiful harbor. By an ingenious feat of engineering, the tides of the sea were harnessed to flush the streets of the city.

But at Passover time Pilate had to come to Jerusalem and make his headquarters in the Tower of Antonia. The city was always in a state of agitation at such times, and the governor brought additional troops with him to be ready for any emergency. His power over the people he governed was almost absolute, but he was strictly responsible to his superiors in Rome for maintaining law and order. Any governor who could not control his province, or showed any sign of losing his grip on it, would promptly be recalled in disgrace.

Reports of Pilate's earlier clashes with the population had already reached Rome, and they had not added to his stature there. He arrived in Jerusalem determined that nothing would mar his reputation further during the coming seven days of the Passover.

He had barely arrived in Jerusalem when he was confronted with the problem of Jesus. The chief priests and elders brought their captive to him early on Friday morning. According to one reckoning, this was the fourteenth day of the Jewish month of Nisan, or the third day of April by our calendar. It is one of the most memorable dates in the history of the world, and it adds to the mystery of the strange story of Jesus of Nazareth that the exact day and year are not entirely certain.

The priests and elders first took Jesus to the Hall of Judgment at the Tower of Antonia. But the Jews would not enter the Hall itself. To them it was a heathen place, and therefore unclean. They could not risk contaminating themselves, especially at the time of Passover. So Pilate, in deference to their scruples, set up his court on the many-colored stones of the pavement outside the Hall. He demanded to know what charge was being brought against Jesus.

"*We found this fellow perverting the nation . . . ,*" the

priests told him. Among themselves, in the Sanhedrin, they had found Jesus guilty of blasphemy according to their own code. But they knew that this would make no impression on Pilate, for whom a violation of Jewish law was of no concern. So the priests shifted the charge to make Jesus look like a threat to Roman rule in Judea. They accused him, falsely, of opposing the payment of tribute to Caesar and of calling himself *Christ a king*.

The priests and elders had condemned Jesus to death, but they did not have the authority to carry out such a sentence. Only Pilate could do that. The strategy of the priests was to persuade the governor that Jesus deserved death according to Roman law, in which case the sentence would certainly be carried out.

The charge that Jesus was calling himself a king was what caught Pilate's attention. It had the smell of sedition about it, and this was something he could not ignore.

Twice he asked Jesus if he were the King of the Jews.

The first time Jesus answered: *"My kingdom is not of this world."*

The second time, he said: *"To this end I was born, and for this cause came I into the world, that I should bear witness to the truth."*

To this Pilate replied: *"What is truth?"*

He may have said it with a shrug. Or a cynical laugh. He has been called "jesting Pilate" because of this question to Jesus, which has been repeated thousands of times since. But we do not know what tone he used when he asked it. All we know is that he then turned back to Jesus' accusers and said to them: *"I find in him no fault at all."*

It was the first of Pilate's public statements that he saw no merit in the charges brought against Jesus. But the priests and elders only pressed their case all the harder. They made another accusation that was shrewdly designed to make the governor think twice about setting Jesus free. *"He stirreth up the people . . . ,"* they said. He was causing unrest throughout the land of Israel, all the way from Galilee to this very place, Jerusalem. A dangerous fellow.

Ordinarily Pilate would have acted with the utmost severity against any agitator brought before him. Roman tolerance ended where rebellion began. But from the first, Pilate showed a curious reluctance to pass judgment on Jesus. Something about the way this man bore himself, the way he spoke, what he said—all this impressed the hard-bitten Roman in a way he probably did not understand himself. One Jewish life more or less meant nothing to Pontius Pilate, but this case, he sensed, was different.

For whatever reason, Pilate did not want to be responsible for the death of Jesus of Nazareth. Now, learning that Jesus was from Galilee, he thought he saw a way of disposing of the case by shifting the decision to somebody else. If Jesus was a Galilean, he must come under the rule of Herod Antipas, who was the tetrarch of Galilee. And Herod was in Jerusalem at this very moment.

Pilate sent Jesus to him.

Herod was pleased. He had heard much about Jesus as a wonder-worker and was eager to meet him. He hoped to have a miracle performed for his special benefit. Jesus had deliberately avoided any encounter with him, calling him *"that fox."* But now he stood before Herod. He stood silent. He answered no questions. As he did throughout the trial, Jesus seemed calmly aloof, almost indifferent to what was going on around him. His destiny was taking its course and he was reconciled to it.

Unable to get any response from him, Herod sent him back to Pilate without passing judgment on him. Probably as a bit of mockery, Herod had Jesus dressed in a *gorgeous robe* before sending him back. "Here's your king," Herod was saying. "Take him. He's your problem."

Now Pilate tried a different tack. It was the custom at Passover time for the authorities to let the people choose a prisoner who would then be released as a gesture of good will. In custody at the time was a notorious criminal named Barabbas, who was a robber, a murderer, and a revolutionary.

He was probably one of the Zealots, and may also have been from Galilee, where so many of the underground fighters came from. Curiously, there is reason to believe that his full name was Jesus Barabbas, or Jesus the son of Abbas.

Pilate decided to give the people a choice of which prisoner should be released to them: Jesus Barabbas or, as he said, *Jesus which is called Christ*. The governor was certain that between the gentle preacher from Galilee and a murderous revolutionary, the choice would not be in doubt.

By this time the morning was well advanced, and there was a crowd around Pilate's outdoor court. This consisted of a raised platform on the open pavement with the governor's official chair on it. Wherever that chair was set up, with Pilate sitting in it, became the seat of Roman authority, the highest tribunal in the land.

The crowd consisted of hangers-on of the nearby Temple, loiterers, and the kind of rabble that swarms together in the streets of a large city whenever anything unusual or exciting goes on. The priests and their followers circulated among these people, stirring them up against Jesus and churning up mob emotion. When Pilate made his offer to them—Barabbas or Jesus—the priestly faction had done its work. The mob immediately shouted: "*Release unto us Barabbas!*"

Pilate was taken aback. He had not expected that response. *"What shall I do then with Jesus which is called the Christ?"* he asked.

The roar came back from the crowd: *"Let him be crucified!"*

And when Pilate said that nothing had been proved against Jesus, the howl of the mob came again and again: *"Crucify him! Crucify him!"*

There were probably some in the crowd who were Zealots and who shouted for the release of Barabbas from patriotic motives. To them the death of Jesus only meant that their man would go free. There may have been others who were genuinely shocked at Jesus' teachings and his defiance of custom and tradition. They may have felt sincerely that he was a menace to society. But the main roar welled up from the mindless emotion of a big city mob manipulated by demagogues.

The roar certainly did not come from the Jews as a people. Only a handful did the shouting. Most of the Jews then in Jerusalem were unaware that Jesus had even been arrested, to say nothing of knowing that he was on trial for his life. The city was jammed with pilgrims from abroad who had never heard of him. There were several million Jews dispersed around the Middle East and elsewhere who had no idea at all of who he was or what he taught. The overwhelming majority of Jews alive in the world at the time of Jesus' trial did not so much as know that he existed.

For Pilate, the immediate concern was to placate the mob that was milling around on the pavement before the Hall of Justice. He now decided to give the mob a taste of the blood it was shouting for. In the hope of calming down the uproar, he ordered Jesus to be scourged. Perhaps that would satisfy them.

So Jesus was stripped and tied to a short post, or pillar,

that forced him to bend over. This made his back a more exposed target for the lash, which was made of leather thongs studded with bits of metal to increase the pain. Under Jewish law, a man could be beaten with no more than forty lashes. In practice, only thirty-nine were ever inflicted, in case there was a mistake in the count. But under the Romans there was no limit to the number of strokes that could be delivered, and this scourging was a Roman one.

How many lashes Jesus suffered is not recorded, but he was probably beaten without mercy. Pilate's soldiers were not disciplined Romans; they were second-rate conscripts from occupied territories, brutal by nature and happy to get their hands on a helpless Jew.

Few forms of punishment were more cruel than scourging. It could tear off the skin until the muscle and bone beneath were exposed, leaving the flesh in shreds. But Pilate's men were not content with this. They had to have a bit of fun with their victim as well. Was this the fellow who was called "King of the Jews"? Well, let's make him look like a king then!

Somewhere they dug up a discarded cloak of purple, the color of royalty. They flung it around Jesus' lacerated shoulders. Then one of them bent a thorny branch into a circle and pressed it down on Jesus' head. That was the crown. The final touch was to clamp his bound hands around a reed or stick. That was the royal scepter.

Then the soldiers cuffed him and spat at him and knelt down before him as if to worship him. *"Hail, King of the Jews!"* they shouted.

Jesus stood bleeding and silent amid the mockery.

Pontius Pilate made one last effort.

He led Jesus out again to face the mob, and he said two words: *"Ecce homo!"*

Perhaps he said it—*"Behold the man!"*—to arouse the compassion of the crowd for this beaten and broken figure. Perhaps he said it with a sneer: "Look at this pathetic creature bleeding in his shabby purple robe and his pitiful crown of thorns. Some king! He's too ridiculous to be a menace to anybody or anything. Turn him loose...."

But the same old roar came back from the crowd: *"Crucify him!"*

Now the chief priests produced a final argument that they knew would bring Pilate up short and force his hand. *"If thou let this man go,"* they told him, *"thou art not Caesar's friend. Whosoever maketh himself a king speaketh against Caesar."*

It was a thrust that hit home.

Pilate knew he could not afford any more official complaints to Rome on his conduct as governor. How would he stand at the court of Tiberius when reports came in that Pontius Pilate was fostering sedition by protecting a Jewish rebel out there in the province of Judea?

On those terms there could no longer be any doubt about Pilate's attitude. For the sake of his career and of his whole future he needed to be in good standing with Caesar. What was the life of another Jewish agitator compared with that? The fate of this Nazarene was of only passing concern at best and would soon be forgotten by everybody, including Pontius Pilate....

In full view of the mob, he washed his hands. This signified that as far as he was concerned the case was now closed. It also showed that he took no responsibility for what was about to happen.

Pilate still thought Jesus innocent, but *he delivered him to be crucified.*

And they took Jesus, and led him away.

At Golgotha, which was also called Calvary, a brief touch of kindness from strangers relieved the terrible grimness of the proceedings.

It was the custom for a group of women from Jerusalem, a kind of Ladies Aid Society, to offer condemned men a last-minute drink to soothe their sufferings. The drink had a narcotic in it, a drug to deaden the senses and lesson the agony that was coming.

When the cup was offered to Jesus, he touched his lips to it and gave it back without drinking. He had determined in the Garden of Gethsemane to drink his own cup of suffering to the dregs.

The business of crucifixion went forward quickly and efficiently. This was a Roman form of punishment, and the soldiers had had plenty of practice at it. Thousands of men had been crucified before these three—the man from Galilee and the two criminals with him—and thousands more would be after them. There would come a time when the Romans crucified so many hundreds of Jews at once that only lack of wood for more crosses called a halt to it.

While it was happening, the crucifixion of Jesus was a routine affair, of interest to only a small group of people:

to the priests and officials who wished to see him dead, and to the little band of obscure men and women who loved him.

It was while he was being nailed to the cross, as it was still stretched on the ground, that Jesus spoke one of the most sublime sentences ever recorded. As the nails were being driven into his hands and feet, he said:
"*Father, forgive them, for they know not what they do.*"

At the moment of his most acute pain and humiliation, Jesus at Golgotha was able to practice the marvelous new doctrine he had first preached in Galilee: *love your enemies, pray for them that persecute you.* . . .

Before the cross was hoisted upright, the soldiers tacked a sign on it above Jesus' head at the orders of Pontius Pilate. The sign read: JESUS OF NAZARETH THE KING OF THE JEWS. It was written in three languages so that every witness and passerby could read it, Hebrew, Greek and Latin.

The chief priests objected. They asked Pilate to change the sign to read *he said* he was the king of the Jews. But Pilate refused to accommodate them. "*What I have written I have written,*" he said.

Once the cross was raised upright with Jesus hanging on it, the soldiers began dividing up his clothes—his head scarf, his sandals, his belt—among themselves. They were entitled to the personal belongings of the men they executed, and they did not wait for their victims to die before collecting this petty loot. Jesus' tunic, or coat, presented a problem. It was all of a piece, woven from top to bottom without a seam. We are not told how Jesus came by this unusual garment. Perhaps the women who followed and supported him had made him a present of it. Perhaps his friends at Bethany, Martha and Mary, wove it for him.

Rather than rip the garment in pieces to divide the cloth among the four of them, the soldiers *cast lots for it,* or rolled dice to see who would get it whole. This went on at the foot of the cross, under the eyes of Jesus.

He could see and hear many who were glad that he was dying, and who scoffed at him as they watched—*"If thou be the Son of God, come down from the cross."* Even one of the criminals who were crucified at his side taunted him (though the robber on his other side expressed sympathy for him). But of his own disciples he saw only one, John, who was with three of the women who followed him from Galilee.

One of them was Mary, his mother.

Not since the beginning of his ministry, not since the wedding feast at Cana, has she been mentioned in the Gospel story of her son. But she is there with him now at Golgotha, as he hangs from a cross in pain and disgrace amid the hoots and mockery of his enemies.

When Jesus saw her at the side of John, the only disciple who dared to come to the crucifixion, he said: *"Woman, behold thy son!"*

To John he said: *"Behold thy mother!"*

From that moment, John took Mary into his home and was a son to her.

Crucifixion was usually a long, lingering death. The sagging position of the victim on the cross pressed the lungs together, making breathing more and more difficult and causing suffocation. The victim gulped continually for air. The blood sank to the lower part of the body. Too little reached the head and heart. Terrible pain and exhaustion racked the whole body. The ultimate cruelty was that this torture would sometimes last for two or three days before the victim was finally released by death.

In the case of Jesus, the ordeal was mercifully short. It lasted about three hours. But how intense his suffering was is revealed by the terrible cry that escaped him toward the end:

"*Eloi, Eloi, lama sabachthani.*"

This was spoken in his mother tongue of Aramaic, and the meaning of it was:

"*My God, my God, why hast thou forsaken me?*"

The words were from a psalm, and they expressed Jesus' human agony and terror at feeling abandoned and alone on the brink of death. At that moment, as Christians believe, Jesus Christ was suffering to the utmost for the sins of the whole world. He had reached the bottom of his cup.

Not long afterward he said, "*I thirst.*" Raging thirst was one of the torments of crucifixion, along with its other agonies. Either out of kindness, or to keep him alive for further suffering, one of the soldiers dipped a sponge in a jar of the tart wine that the troops always had with them. On a long stick the sponge was raised to Jesus' mouth, and he drank. This was not the drugged drink he had refused before, but ordinary wine for his thirst.

Two more sayings are recorded from Jesus on the cross. As he felt the end coming, he said:

"*It is finished.*"

This announced that his work was done. His mission was ended. The wave of deep despair that engulfed him had passed, and he no longer felt abandoned and alone. Now, instead, he called out:

"*Father, into thy hands I commend my spirit.*"

Then he died.

Ordinarily the body of a criminal would be left to hang on the cross indefinitely, whether he was alive or dead. But this was a Friday, and the Sabbath would begin at sundown. And this year the Sabbath coincided with the beginning of the Passover.

It was now about three o'clock in the afternoon, and the pious could not tolerate that bodies should be hanging from crosses during the Sabbath. The Jewish authorities demanded that the death of all three men on Golgotha be hastened.

This was done by a set procedure called the *"crurifragium,"* which meant breaking the legs of the victim below the knee with a club. When the support of the legs was gone, the added strain on the arms constricted the chest muscles violently. The pressure on the lungs then made breathing impossible.

The soldiers used their clubs on the two robbers.

But when they came to Jesus, they found he was already dead. His legs were not broken. Instead, one of the soldiers, to be sure he was really dead, took a spear and thrust it into his side. An eyewitness, who may have been the disciple John himself, saw both water and blood flow from the wound.

By custom, the body of anyone who was crucified would be buried in a potter's field or simply thrown into the nearest ditch. This did not happen to Jesus because of a man named Joseph, who came from a town called Arimathea. He went to Pilate and obtained permission to take Jesus' body from the cross and bury it properly.

Joseph of Arimathea was a wealthy member of the Sanhedrin, but *a good man and just.* He was a disciple of Jesus, like a small number of other rich and prominent Jews, and he had taken no part in the persecution of the prophet from Galilee. Even now, it took courage for him to come forward as a follower of Jesus and assume responsibility for his burial.

Near to Calvary was a garden in which stood a sepulcher, or tomb, carved out of rock. This was to have been Joseph's own burial place. But now he brought Jesus' body there, wrapped it in fine linen, and laid it in the tomb. Then he had a large stone rolled into the entrance to close it, and left, because by now night was coming on. The Sabbath was beginning, and all activity ceased.

AT FIRST, at the crucifixion, Mary Magdalene had stood watching *afar off* with the other women who followed Jesus from Galilee. Then as the hours wore on, she drew closer and closer to the cross. Finally she was standing under it at the side of Mary the Mother.

Ever since Jesus miraculously cured her of a severe emotional sickness, which was probably a kind of insanity—he had *cast seven devils out of her*—she had been one of his most dedicated followers. Of all the women who attended Jesus, this Mary from the town of Magdala has come down through the centuries as a more vivid and memorable personality than any of the others.

She has been pictured in painting, song and story as the prototype, the model, for the "fallen" woman who repents of her sins and then leads a life of piety and virtue. This is, apparently, an immensely appealing idea to one generation after the other, and no one has ever personified it more effectively than the character who has been given the name of Mary Magdalene.

She has been made the patron saint of penitents. Artists like Titian and Correggio have painted her, always portraying her as young and beautiful. She is usually shown with long hair and with a box of ointments. Books and plays have been written about her. Homes that shelter delinquent girls and former prostitutes are often called Magdalene Asylums in her honor.

All this is an error, without foundation.

The only reliable record we have of Mary Magdalene is in the Gospels, and none of them describes her as a sinful woman who reformed. They report only that Jesus drove evil spirits out of her. This does not prove, or even imply, that she was unchaste. It only suggests that she was emotionally disturbed.

Without any real basis, Mary Magdalene has been identified with another woman who was indeed wicked, and who came into contact with Jesus and admired him greatly. This woman is never named. She is described several times as *a sinner*, so the assumption has been made that she was sexually loose, a prostitute (though there are, of course, many other ways for a woman to sin). Once, when Jesus was at supper, she bathed his feet in ointments and kissed them to show her admiration and respect for him.

When both she and Jesus were reproved for this incident, he told a parable in her defense and added one of his most lovely and lasting sayings: *"Her sins, which are many, are forgiven; for she loved much . . ."*

"Mary called Magdalene" is first mentioned in Luke immediately following this story of the nameless woman *which was a sinner*. The two were somehow merged and became one personality. The myth-makers seized on the character of the one and the name of the other and interchanged them. The result has been the unfading legend of Mary Magdalene as the symbol of all fallen women who see the light, renounce the past, and with upturned eyes and shining faces walk the path of virtue.

But Mary Magdalene's true claim to immortality, as the Gospels give it, is far more impressive than the sentimental fantasy that has been woven around her. It is, in fact, awesome.

She was the first to see the resurrected Christ.

When the body of Jesus was taken down from the cross and carried away, the women from Galilee followed it to the tomb and saw where it was laid. They went away, then, to make ready for the last service they could offer. They went to prepare spices and ointments for embalming the body. But because of the Sabbath, they did not return to the sepulcher until the first day of the week, which we call Sunday.

Mary Magdalene came early, *when it was yet dark*. She was astonished to see the great stone rolled away from the entrance—and the tomb empty.

In her bewilderment and dismay, Mary Magdalene turned and ran for help. She found two of the disciples to tell her story to: Peter, and *the disciple whom Jesus loved*. This was John, and his Gospel tells the story of the Resurrection as vividly as any.

On hearing Mary's news, the two men immediately sped for the sepulcher, which was evidently close by. John outran Peter and got there first, probably because he was the younger of the two. He stooped down and peered into the entrance of the tomb, but did not go in. He could see the linen burial clothes lying on the floor.

Peter, impetuous as always, went right into the tomb as soon as he reached it. He observed the discarded linen also, and noticed another detail. The napkin that had been wrapped around Jesus' head when he was buried was not *lying with the linen clothes, but wrapped together in a place by itself*. (These striking details became evidence later that the body was not stolen away by the disciples and hidden. If that had happened, would those who robbed the tomb have paused to remove the burial garments, fold them, and put them neatly to one side?)

The two men, satisfied that the body of Jesus had somehow vanished from the tomb, went away to think over what they had seen. Mary Magdalene stayed behind. She lingered at the entrance of the tomb, weeping. She could not resist the impulse to look inside again, and she stooped down to do so.

This time she saw two angels dressed in white and they were sitting at the head and feet of where Jesus had been laid. They asked her why she was crying. *"Because they have taken away my Lord,"* she said, *"and I know not where they have laid him."*

Then she noticed a figure in the garden where the sepulcher was located. Mary thought it was the gardener. He asked her why she was crying and what she was looking for. "Sir," she said, "if you know where he is, please tell me and I will take him away."

Instead of answering, the man she thought was the gardener spoke her name: *"Mary."*

At once she knew it was Jesus.

She said: *"Rabboni!"* which meant Master, or Teacher.

In all four Gospels Mary Magdalene is present at the empty tomb on that morning we now call Easter. But

Matthew, Mark and Luke also describe other incidents related to the day. One of these involves a conference of the chief priests and Pharisees with Pontius Pilate shortly after the crucifixion.

They told him that Jesus had predicted he would rise again on the third day, or Sunday. They feared his disciples would come by night and steal the body away and then *say to the people, "He is risen from the dead," so the last error shall be worse than the first.*

Pilate had already checked with the officer in charge of the execution, a centurion, and made sure that Jesus was dead. For a practical Roman like the governor, that ended the matter completely and he wished to hear no more about it. He told the petitioners to set their own guard around the tomb if they wanted to protect the body. He, Pilate, was not going to give them any of his soldiers for the purpose. So the Jewish authorities put their own armed watch around the sepulcher.

The precaution accomplished nothing.

The figures in shining white, the angels that Mary Magdalene had seen at the tomb, were reported by others as well. Confronted with them, the guards were helpless. *They did shake and become as dead men,* powerless to prevent whatever it was that happened at the grave of Jesus during the night.

Other women from Galilee, we are told, also appeared there with Mary Magdalene, bearing spices and ointments for the embalming. They too *trembled and were amazed* at what they found and at the words of the shining strangers:

"He is not here. He is risen."

The words have echoed and re-echoed joyously around the world since, but at the time they caused mostly shock, consternation and disbelief.

The priests and elders were dumbfounded at the news,

and called a conference in panic to question the watch. When they were satisfied that the body of Jesus had indeed disappeared in some way that could not be explained, they bribed the soldiers *with large money* to spread a lie. They were to say that Jesus had been taken away by his disciples during the night while they, the soldiers, were asleep. *So they took the money and did as they were taught,* and their story has not died out even today.

But the disciples were as astonished at the news as everyone else, and as skeptical. Even Peter and John, who were first at the empty tomb, simply went home afterward, at a loss as to what to do about this unexpected turn of events. When the women first spread the news it was received with blank incredulity. Thomas, one of the twelve, refused to believe even when other disciples told him they themselves had seen Jesus. Doubting Thomas would not be persuaded until he personally touched the holes left by the nails and felt the wound made by the spear. He did this at the invitation of Christ himself on the eighth day after the crucifixion, when the risen Lord appeared before him.

So whatever happened at the tomb could hardly have been the work of the disciples. And since the women had come bearing spices to embalm him, they clearly had no idea he would be risen and gone. Jesus had repeatedly said he would return from the grave, but nobody believed him.

He had great difficulty convincing his followers, even when he reappeared before them repeatedly as a living person. They thought he was a ghost. Besides letting them touch him to prove he was, as he said, *flesh and bones* and not a spirit, he sat down at table and ate and drank with them.

His disciples recorded no fewer than ten of these appearances. Sometimes he would join them as a stranger and be unrecognized until he chose to reveal himself. Sometimes he would suddenly materialize in their midst. One moment he was not there. The next moment he was standing among them.

"*Peace!*" would be his greeting when he showed himself after his Resurrection. "*Peace be unto you.*"

When he appeared among his beloved fishermen on the Sea of Galilee, he seemed as human as before, as much their comrade and companion as he had been before Golgotha. And once again he served them well in their trade by helping them make a good catch.

Peter, John, Thomas and some others were fishing at night. Their luck was bad. They were not far from land when they heard a voice calling to them. Somebody they did not recognize was asking if they had caught anything. They said that so far they had caught nothing at all.

The stranger on the shore told them to cast their net on the right side of the boat. They did so—and made such a haul that they could hardly get the net back into the boat.

John turned to Peter and said: "*It is the Lord.*"

At this, Peter, who had been fishing naked, put on his fisherman's tunic, jumped into the water, and made for the shore, which was only about a hundred yards off. The others followed in the boat, dragging along the net which now held one hundred and fifty-three fishes.

They found Jesus cooking fish over a fire of coals. "*Come and eat,*" he said to them, and served fresh-cooked fish and bread to all hands. There in the open, on the seashore, as the dawn was breaking over Galilee, the rugged fishermen and the risen Lord made a savory meal of it together.

For believing Christians, this is an entrancing incident, and one that illustrates with a special vividness the mystery of Christ's dual personality.

What could be more warm and human than the picture of Jesus as chef at a seaside cookout, whipping up an impromptu breakfast for some old friends just in from a hard night's work? (Where did he get the fish or the coals for his fire? Another of his friendly little miracles, perhaps.)

But this informal and affable person who calls out cordially, *"Come and eat!"* is also the Son of God. He is God in his own right, newly returned from the grave. Even as they enjoy his hospitality, the fishermen sense this and feel a certain constraint in his presence. *Knowing it was the Lord,* they do not dare ask him to identify himself or inquire how he happened to be there.

Like so much else in the story of Jesus, this cannot be comprehended by reason. As with the Resurrection itself, rational explanation is hopeless. All that can be said is what the apostle Paul wrote in one of his letters to the early church at Corinth: *"Behold, I show you a mystery..."*

But the Resurrection, as the New Testament tells it, is such an overwhelming event that there have been many attempts to explain it, or explain it away. For Christians the matter is fairly simple: Christ was crucified for the sins of the world, died, was buried, and rose up again. He then ascended into heaven to sit on the right hand of God the Father. He will come again on Judgment Day, at the end of the world, to punish the wicked and reward the righteous with everlasting life.

For those who accept this as part of their faith, the Resurrection is "the central fact in all history," as a great French churchman called it. The whole of Christian doctrine depends on it. (*"If Christ be not raised, your faith is vain . . .*") When skeptics ask, as they do about the other miracles, how it could be possible for God to die as a man and come back to life, believers have the same answer: What is unimaginable to man is easily possible to God.

At any rate, millions around the world, in all religions and at all times, have found that implausibility is no hindrance to belief. Tertullian, one of the most brilliant and learned of the early Church fathers, justified his faith by saying: "*Credo, quia absurdam*"—"I believe because it is absurd." Another version of Tertullian's saying is: "It is certain because it is impossible."

Many, of course, do not believe precisely because the matter seems both absurd and impossible. They contend that the Resurrection did not happen as the Bible tells it because no such thing *could* happen. They argue that Jesus, a man and only a man, did not die on the cross. He was taken down from it while still alive, and revived by his friends. After making a few appearances, he lived out the rest of his natural life in obscurity. His followers spread the fraudulent story of his return from the grave and his ascent into heaven.

This ignores the fact that the soldiers in charge of Jesus' execution undoubtedly knew their business. They knew when a man was dead and when he wasn't. It ignores Pilate's query to the officer in charge, who assured him that Jesus was indeed dead. It also does not account for the acceptance of his death by the disciples and by the women from Galilee. They were much closer to the event than later commentators, and they had no doubt that Jesus had died.

Another argument goes that Jesus did indeed die on the cross, but that he stayed dead. The reports of his disciples that he was seen alive afterward were based on illusion. Mary Magdalene and the other women at the tomb; Peter,

John, Thomas and the others who reported seeing and touching him; the fishermen at the Sea of Galilee that night who ate and talked with him; the disciples who said they saw him ascend into heaven—they were all under the influence of some kind of hysteria brought on by grief and hope. They were victims of hallucination and religious delirium.

Some skeptics have gone further. They say that the entire story of Jesus, from his birth to his death and everything between, is a myth. He never lived at all. Jesus Christ was, and is, a product of the human imagination, like Osiris, Mithras, Attis and Dionysus. He is part of the world's store of mythology and legend. The figure that fiction created and called Jesus answered some deep-seated psychic need of the human race. He has endured because he was a synthesis, or weaving together, of many myths and legends that have appealed to the masses through the ages.

The idea that Jesus never really existed gets support from the fact that there are no known contemporary records about him. The idea is not new. It is not merely the product of modern doubt and disbelief. Jesus had not been dead seventy years when a cult developed which maintained that he had never been a man, but only a phantom, a spirit. People who believed this were called Docetists, and there have been variations of this idea ever since, down to our own time. But the notion that Jesus Christ never existed is now regarded as extreme and unwarranted. It has few serious defenders.

Mystery still surrounds much of the human life of Jesus. It continues to resist clarification by scholars and investigators. The gaps and obscurities remain. It is possible that some great breakthrough of research may yet occur. Some undreamed-of manuscript may suddenly be uncovered that will throw startling new light on Jesus as a person and on his life on earth.

There was hope of this in 1947 when a Bedouin shepherd boy, looking for a stray lamb, stumbled on a cache of forgotten manuscripts in a cave near the Dead Sea. At first it was thought these ancient scrolls would provide a direct link to Jesus and his time, and would tell us more about him and the world in which he moved than was ever known before. The Dead Sea Scrolls are still being studied, but as yet they have produced no sensational revelations. We know basically no more about Jesus than before the scrolls were discovered. He remains as enigmatic and mysterious as ever.

On the other hand, when modern research does unearth something related to events described in the Bible, the discovery has tended to support the Scriptures. The digs of archeologists in the Holy Land have enriched our knowledge of Biblical times, and continue to do so. None of the discoveries has yet seriously contradicted a biblical reference. Time after time, the scriptural account of a given event has been supported by contemporary excavations.

Still, no amount of digging into the ground or analyzing old manuscripts will ever prove, once and for all, that Jesus was the Son of God and that the Resurrection actually happened. But if, as the skeptics say, those things are not true, a wonderfully strange thing has happened. The effect on the world has been exactly the same as if they were true.

Nothing else that ever happened has had such enormous consequences, and it can almost be said that the spread of Christianity is more miraculous if the story of the Resurrection is not true than if it is.

At any rate, the little band of Jesus' followers certainly

believed that he came back from the grave. Acting on that belief, and inspired by it, they launched a movement that would sweep the world.

When they began they were only about one hundred and twenty men and women meeting in a room in Jerusalem. The first apostles were, as the Bible itself calls them, *unlearned and ignorant men.* Their leader had just been executed in the most degrading and disgraceful way, as a common criminal. What they preached sounded like utter nonsense to most of the people who heard them. They, and the beginning few who believed them, were brutally persecuted as heretics, subversives and madmen. They were tortured, fed to wild animals, crucified, burned, beheaded, slaughtered. At first by the score, then by the hundreds, and then by the thousands.

Yet, in the end, it was not the mighty Roman Empire that prevailed over the pitiful little gaggle of fanatics who called themselves Christians. Instead, it was the Empire that crumbled and fell to pieces while the Christians steadily increased their numbers until their doctrine dominated the entire Western world.

The parable about the sower whose seed fell on good ground and brought forth its fruit a hundredfold became reality far beyond the imagination of the simple Galileans who first heard Jesus tell the story. And the alarm expressed by the Pharisees about the popularity of Jesus and his doctrine—*"Behold, the world has gone after him"*—was justified on a scale they could not have conceived of when they set themselves to oppose him at the start.

The impact of the obscure Jew named Jesus on the world has been called "the most surprising fact in history." It could not possibly have been predicted. It was not realized while it was happening. It is not easily accounted for even now when it has been an established fact for many centuries.

Certainly a very great factor in his appeal has been the mystical love and adoration which his personality has been able to inspire in so many millions over so many years. His sayings and teachings opened the way to a more abundant life for all who chose to follow him. His doctrine offered comfort and joy to all, excluding none. It made no distinction as to sex, color, caste or social status. *"Come unto me all ye that labor and are heavy laden,"* he said, *"and I will give you rest."*

He preached early what the world is only now struggling toward. "His deceptively simple gospel of universal brotherhood and love was so revolutionary," a secular historian has written, "that it has taken many centuries to realize its implications, and merely to begin to effect them in political and economic life."

The revolutionary content in Jesus' teaching has always attracted the young, and more so today, perhaps, than ever before. It is usually overlooked how young Jesus was, and how youthful his attitude was. He was only twelve, after all, when he stood up to the learned doctors in the Temple and freely expressed his opinions before them. He was a young man when he defied convention and drove the money-changers from the Temple courtyard.

He loved the idea of childhood and youth. He often addressed his disciples as *"Children."* It was for him a word of warm affection, and it is sometimes translated as *"young men"* or *"young people."* He spoke of his followers as *"children of the Kingdom."*

He was hardly more than thirty when he died.

"In the best sense of the word, Jesus was a radical," the Protestant bishop Phillips Brooks has pointed out. "His religion has so long been identified with conservatism—often with conservatism of the obstinate and unyielding sort—that it is almost startling for us sometimes to remember that all of the conservatism of his own times was against him; that it was the young, free, restless, sanguine, progressive part of the people who flocked to him."

The radicalism of Jesus' teaching had little to do with politics or government, which seemed to be matters of indifference to him. It involved deep-going revisions of how people thought and felt. This, he taught, would inevitably govern how they related to each other and to God. Unless people changed their ways of thinking, feeling and reacting, there could be no universal brotherhood and peace.

His sayings and teachings pointed the way, the only way.

The new commandment he gave his disciples in the upper room in Jerusalem—". . . *that ye love one another* . . ."—was the key to his Kingdom.

The words that I speak unto you
They are spirit and they are life.
—JOHN 6:63

Know ye not that ye are the temple of God, and that the Spirit of God dwelleth in you?

I CORINTHIANS 3:16

Jesus said unto him, Thou shalt love the Lord thy God with all thy heart, and with all thy soul, and with all thy mind.
This is the first and great commandment.
And the second is like unto it; Thou shalt love thy neighbor as thyself.
On these two commandments hang all the law and the prophets.

MATTHEW 22:37–40

Are not five sparrows sold for two farthings, and not one of them is forgotten before God? But even the very hairs of your head are all numbered. Fear not therefore: ye are of more value than many sparrows.

LUKE 12:6–7

And why take ye thought for raiment? Consider
    the lilies of the field, how they grow;
    they toil not, neither do they spin:
And yet I say unto you, That even Solomon
    in all his glory was not arrayed like one
    of these.
Wherefore, if God so clothe the grass of the
    field, which today is and tomorrow is
    cast into the oven, shall he not much more
    clothe you, O ye of little faith?
MATTHEW 6:28–30

Judge not, and ye shall not be judged: condemn
    not, and ye shall not be condemned: forgive,
    and ye shall be forgiven:
LUKE 6:37

Woe unto the world because of offences! for
    it must needs be that offences come; but woe to
    that man by whom the offence cometh!
MATTHEW 18:7

And I say unto you, Ask, and it shall be given
 you; seek, and ye shall find; knock, and it
 shall be opened unto you.
For every one that asketh receiveth; and he
 that seeketh findeth; and to him that knocketh
 it shall be opened.
LUKE 11:9–10

When thou makest a dinner or a supper, call not
 thy friends, nor thy brethren, neither thy
 kinsmen, nor thy rich neighbours; lest they also
 bid thee in return, and a repayment be made
 thee.
But when thou makest a feast, call the poor,
 the maimed, the lame, the blind:
And thou shalt be blessed; for they cannot
 repay thee; for thou shalt be repaid
 at the resurrection of the just.
LUKE 14:12–14

Therefore if thine enemy hunger, feed him; if he
    thirst, give him drink: for in so doing thou
    shalt heap coals of fire on his head.
Be not overcome by evil, but overcome evil
    with good.

ROMANS 12:20–21

Why beholdest thou the mote that is in thy
    brother's eye, but considerest not the beam
    that is in thine own eye?
Thou hypocrite, first cast out the beam out of
    thine own eye; and then shalt thou see clearly
    to cast out the mote out of thy brother's eye.

MATTHEW 7:3, 5

Ye shall know the truth, and the truth
    shall make you free.

JOHN 8:32

Beware of false prophets, which come to you
    in sheep's clothing, but inwardly they are
    ravening wolves.
Ye shall know them by their fruits. Do men
    gather grapes of thorns, or figs of thistles?
Even so every good tree bringeth forth good
    fruit; but a corrupt tree bringeth forth
    evil fruit...
Every tree that bringeth not forth good
    fruit is hewn down, and cast into the fire.

                              MATTHEW 7:15–17, 19

Let all bitterness, and wrath, and anger, and
    clamour, and evil speaking, be put away from
    you, with all malice.
And be ye kind one to another . . .

                              EPHESIANS 4:31–32

... ye ought to support the weak, and to remember the words of the Lord Jesus, how he said, It is more blessed to give than to receive.

THE ACTS 20:35

God is not the God of the dead, but of the living.

MATTHEW 22:32

Brethren, whatsoever things are true, whatsoever things are honest, whatsoever things are just, whatsoever things are pure, whatsoever things are lovely, whatsoever things are of good report; if there be any virtue, and if there be any praise, think on these things.

PHILIPPIANS 4:8

He attacks the Establishment
of His time — and ours ...

Children, how hard it is for them that trust
   in riches to enter into the Kingdom of God!
                                    MARK 10:24

Beware of the scribes [lawyers and leaders], which desire
   to walk in long robes, and love greetings in the
   markets, and the highest seats in the synagogues,
   and the chief rooms at feasts;
Who devour widows' houses, and for a show make
   long prayers: the same shall receive greater
   damnation.
                                    LUKE 20:46–47

Woe unto you, scribes and Pharisees, hypocrites!
. . . Outwardly ye appear righteous unto men, but
   within ye are full of hypocrisy and iniquity.
                                    MATTHEW 23:27–28

... they bind heavy burdens that are grievously hard to bear on the shoulders of others; but they themselves will not move a finger to help carry the load.

MATTHEW 23:4

... they be blind leaders of the blind. And if the blind lead the blind, both shall fall into the ditch.

MATTHEW 15:14

This people draweth nigh unto me with their mouth, and honoureth me with their lips; but their heart is far from me.

MATTHEW 15:8

For the love of money is the root of all evil . . .
>   1 TIMOTHY 6:10

Lay not up for yourself treasures upon
    earth, where moth and rust doth corrupt,
    and where thieves break through and steal:
But lay up for yourselves treasures in
    heaven, where neither moth nor rust doth
    corrupt, and where thieves do not break
    through nor steal:
For where your treasure is, there will your
    heart be also.
>   MATTHEW 6:19–21

For we brought nothing into this world, and it
    is certain we can carry nothing out.
>   1 TIMOTHY 6:7

The heart of His message:
Love, Brotherhood, Peace ...

He that loveth not knoweth not God;
   for God is love.

I JOHN 4:8

Though I speak with the tongues of men and of
   angels, and have not charity [love], I am become as
   sounding brass, or a tinkling cymbal.
And though I have the gift of prophecy, and
   understand all mysteries, and all knowledge;
   and though I have all faith, so that I could
   remove mountains, and have not charity, I am
   nothing.
And though I bestow all my goods to feed the
   poor, and though I give my body to be burned,
   and have not charity, it profiteth me nothing.

I CORINTHIANS 13:1–3

If a man say, I love God, and hateth his
 brother, he is a liar: for he that loveth
 not his brother whom he hath seen, how can
 he love God whom he hath not seen?
And this commandment have we from him,
 That he who loveth God love his brother
 also.
I JOHN 4:20–21

Owe no man anything, but to love one
 another: for he that loveth another
 hath fulfilled the law.
ROMANS 13:8

... guide our feet into the way of peace.
LUKE 1:79

Let us therefore follow after the things which
    make for peace, and things wherewith one may
    buoy up another.

ROMANS 14:19

Follow peace with all men, and holiness, without
    which no man shall see the Lord.

HEBREWS 12:14

And into whatsoever house ye enter, first say:
    Peace be to this house.

LUKE 10:5

Parables and Prayers

HE TELLS THE STORY OF THE SON WHO LEFT HOME—AND CAME BACK AGAIN

A certain man had two sons:
    And the younger of them said to his father, "Father, give me the portion of goods that is due me." And the father divided his goods between his sons.
And not many days after the younger son gathered his portion together, and took his journey into a far country, and there wasted his substance with riotous living.
And when he had spent all, there arose a mighty famine in that land; and he began to be in want.
And he went and joined himself to a citizen of that country; and he sent him into his fields to feed swine.
And he would fain have filled his belly with the husks that the swine did eat: and no man gave unto him.
And when he came to himself, he said, "How many hired servants of my father's have bread enough and to spare, and I perish of hunger!
"I will arise and go to my father, and will say unto him, 'Father, I have sinned against heaven, and before thee.'
"And am no more worthy to be called thy son: make me as one of thy hired servants."
And he arose, and came to his father. But when he was yet a great way off, his father saw him, and had compassion, and ran, and fell on his neck, and kissed him.
And the son said unto him, "Father, I have sinned against heaven, and in thy sight, and am no more worthy to be called thy son."
But the father said to his servants, "Bring forth

the best robe, and put it on him, and put a ring on his hand, and shoes on his feet:

"And bring hither the fatted calf, and kill it; and let us eat, and be merry.

"For this my son was dead, and is alive again; he was lost, and is found." And they began to be merry.

Now his elder son was in the field: and as he came and drew nigh to the house, he heard music and dancing.

And he called one of the servants, and asked what these things meant.

And he said unto him, "Thy brother is come; and thy father hath killed the fatted calf, because he hath received him safe and sound."

And he was angry, and would not go in: therefore came his father out, and entreated him.

And he answering said to his father, "Lo, these many years do I serve thee, neither transgressed I at any time thy commandment; and yet thou never gavest me even a goat, that I might make merry with my friends.

"But as soon as this thy son was come, which hath devoured thy living with harlots, thou hast killed for him the fatted calf."

And the father said unto him, "Son, thou art ever with me, and all that I have is thine.

"It was right that we should make merry, and be glad: for this thy brother was dead, and is alive again; and was lost, and is found."

LUKE 15:11–32

THE SERMON ON THE MOUNT

And seeing the multitudes, he went up into a
    mountain: and when he was set, his disciples
    came unto him:
And he opened his mouth, and taught them,
    saying,
Blessed are the poor in spirit: for theirs
    is the kingdom of heaven.
Blessed are they that mourn: for they shall
    be comforted.
Blessed are the meek: for they shall inherit
    the earth.
Blessed are they which do hunger and thirst
    after righteousness: for they shall be filled.
Blessed are the merciful: for they shall obtain
    mercy.
Blessed are the pure in heart: for they shall
    see God.
Blessed are the peacemakers: for they shall
    be called the children of God.
Blessed are they which are persecuted for
    righteousness' sake: for theirs is the kingdom
    of heaven.

MATTHEW 5:1–10

THE LORD'S PRAYER

After this manner therefore pray ye: Our Father
    which art in heaven, Hallowed be thy name.
Thy kingdom come. Thy will be done in earth, as
    it is in heaven.
Give us this day our daily bread.
And forgive us our debts, as we forgive our
    debtors.
And lead us not into temptation, but deliver us
    from evil: For thine is the kingdom, and the
    power, and the glory, forever. Amen.

MATTHEW 6:9–13

HE CALLS A LITTLE CHILD UNTO HIM . . .

And Jesus called a little child unto him, and
    set him in the midst of them.
And said, Verily I say unto you, Except ye be
    converted and become as little children, ye
    shall not enter into the kingdom of heaven.
Whosoever therefore shall humble himself as
    this little child, the same is greatest in the
    kingdom of heaven.
And whoso shall receive one such little child
    in my name receiveth me.
But whoso shall offend one of these little ones
    which believe in me, it were better for him that
    a millstone were hanged about his neck, and that
    he were drowned in the depth of the sea.
                                MATTHEW 18:2–6

". . . YE HAVE DONE IT UNTO ME."

For I was hungry, and ye gave me meat: I was
 thirsty, and ye gave me drink: I was a stranger,
 and ye took me in:
Naked, and ye clothed me: I was sick, and ye
 visited me: I was in prison, and ye came unto
 me.
Then shall the righteous answer him, saying, Lord,
 when saw we thee hungry, and fed thee? or thirsty
 and gave thee drink?
When saw we thee a stranger, and took thee in?
 or naked, and clothed thee?
Or when saw we thee sick, or in prison, and came
 unto thee?
And the King shall answer and say unto them, Verily
 I say unto you, Inasmuch as ye have done it unto one
 of the least of these my brethren, ye have done it
 unto me.

MATTHEW 25:35–40

"A Certain Rich Man..."

And he spake a parable unto them, saying, The
   ground of a certain rich man brought forth
   plentifully:
And he thought within himself, saying, What
   shall I do because I have no room where to
   bestow my fruits?
And he said, This will I do: I will pull down
   my barns, and build greater; and there will I
   bestow all my fruits and my goods.
And I will say to my soul, Soul, thou hast
   much goods laid up for many years; take thine
   ease, eat, drink, and be merry.
But God said unto him, Thou fool, this night
   thy soul shall be required of thee: then whose
   shall those things be, which thou hast
   provided?
So is he that layeth up treasure for himself,
   and is not rich toward God.

LUKE 12:16–21

THE PHARISEE AND THE PUBLICAN

And he spake this parable unto certain which
    trusted in themselves that they were righteous,
    and despised others:
Two men went up into the temple to pray; the
    one a Pharisee, and the other a publican.
The Pharisee stood and prayed thus with himself,
    "God, I thank thee, that I am not as other men
    are, extortioners, unjust, adulterers, or even
    as this publican.
"I fast twice in the week, I give a tenth of all
    that I possess to the Temple."
And the publican, standing afar off, would not
    lift up so much as his eyes unto heaven, but
    smote upon his breast, saying, "God be merciful
    to me a sinner."
I tell you, this man went down to his house
    justified rather than the other; for every one
    that exalteth himself shall be abased; and he
    that humbleth himself shall be exalted.

LUKE 18:9–14

THE HOUSE BUILT UPON A ROCK

Therefore whosoever heareth these sayings of
    mine, and doeth them, I will liken him unto
    a wise man, which built his house upon a rock:
And the rain descended, and the floods came,
    and the winds blew, and beat upon that house;
    and it fell not: for it was founded upon a
    rock.
And every one that heareth these sayings of
    mine, and doeth them not, shall be likened
    unto a foolish man, which built his house
    upon the sand:
And the rain descended, and the floods came,
    and the winds blew, and beat upon that house;
    and it fell: and great was the fall of it.

MATTHEW 7:24–27